What I wish you knew

LETTERS FROM OUR DAUGHTERS' LIVES, AND EXPERT ADVICE ON STAYING CONNECTED

In *What I Wish You Knew,* you'll find expert insight and caring advice from psychologists and educators who specialize in girls' issues:

DR. EVELYN BASSOFF is a practicing psychologist and author of *Mothers and Daughters: Loving and Letting Go* and *Cherishing Our Daughters: How Parents Can Raise Girls to Become Confident Women.*

DR. RONI COHEN-SANDLER is the author of *"I'm Not Mad, I Just Hate You!"* and is a clinical psychologist specializing in the issues of women and adolescent girls.

DR. LYNN PONTON, author of *The Romance of Risk: Why Teenagers Do the Things They Do* and *The Sex Lives of Teenagers,* is a psychoanalyst and professor at the University of California in San Francisco.

MS. VIRGINIA BEANE RUTTER is the author of *Celebrating Girls: Nurturing and Empowering Our Daughters* and *Embracing Persephone: How to Be the Mother You Want for the Daughter You Cherish.* She is also a practicing marriage and family therapist and certified Jungian analyst, specializing in feminine psychology.

DR. LYNDA MADISON is director of psychological services at Children's Hospital in Omaha, Nebraska. She is also the author of *Keep Talking: A Mother-Daughter Guide to the Preteen Years* and *Parenting with Purpose,* as well as a practicing psychologist.

DR. JOANN DEAK is author of *How Girls Thrive: An Essential Guide for Educators (and Parents)* and co-editor of *The Book of Hopes and Dreams for Girls and Young Women.* She is the founder of The DEAK Group, a consulting service for schools and parents, and has been a teacher, school psychologist, and counselor in private practice.

DR. CAROL EAGLE, author of *All That She Can Be: Helping Your Daughter Maintain Her Self-Esteem,* is the former head of the Department of Child and Adolescent Psychology at Montefiore Medical Center in New York. She has run a group-therapy program for 11- to 13-year-old girls for many years.

Published by Pleasant Company Publications
For information, address: Book Editor, Pleasant Company Publications,
8400 Fairway Place, P.O. Box 620998, Middleton, WI 53562.

Printed in the United States of America
01 02 03 04 05 06 07 08 STR 10 9 8 7 6 5 4 3 2

Editorial Direction: Therese Kauchak
Editorial Consultant: Amy Lynch, editor, *Daughters*™
Cover Photography: Model Team, Ocean Grove, NJ
Photography Art Direction: John Merriman
Cover Calligraphy: Lilla Rogers
Art Direction and Design: Julie Mierkiewicz, Lynne Wells
Production: Kendra Pulvermacher, Janette Sowinski
Special Thanks: Harpeth Hall School, Hume-Fogg Academic Magnet
High School, National Association of Anorexia Nervosa and
Associated Disorders

What I wish you knew : letters from our daughters' lives, and expert
advice on staying connected/ [from the editors of American Girl].
p. cm.
Includes index.
ISBN 1-58485-329-8
1. Daughters. 2. Mothers and daughters. I. American girl
(Middleton, Wis.)
HQ777 .W48 2001
306.874'3—dc21   2001018512

Contents

"I have no one to discuss my problems with. Ever since I hit puberty,
I've felt like an outcast to my father. I'm ashamed to show that my
breasts are growing and that I got my period. I've tried talking to my
mom, but she doesn't understand what I'm going through. Sometimes
I cry myself to sleep. I feel more comfortable talking to my friends than
I do my parents. I'd like to be able to talk to my mom and dad."

age 13

American Girl

Dear Parents,

Your daughter has a lot on her mind, but she doesn't always know how to tell you—even when she really wants to. For the last 15 years, American Girl has been learning about girls' fondest dreams and greatest worries through their thoughtful and revealing letters. We thought it was time to share those letters with you. To offer the widest diversity of girls' voices we partnered with Web site SmartGirl.com, and for the best advice on how parents can connect with their daughters we looked to *Daughters* Newsletter.

Each chapter in *What I Wish You Knew* opens with insight from a therapist or educator, followed by letters from girls and advice on how you can help your daughter if she has similar experiences. Additional practical tips close each chapter.

Every time we dive into a treasure trove of girls' letters, we are enlightened and feel that we know girls even better than we did before. We hope this book does the same for you—and makes you feel more connected to the important American girls in your life.

Sincerely,
The Editors at American Girl®

Daughters

Dear Parents,

When I was an adolescent, my father used to say to me, "Remember who you are." It drove me crazy. Like most girls that age, I was bent on becoming someone I wasn't yet and, sometimes, someone my parents might not want me to be. Today, however, I see how my dad's words bolstered me when I was faced with difficult decisions. In fact, his words spring to mind when I talk with my own daughters. What I want for each of them (and, no doubt, what you want for your daughter) is precisely what my dad wanted for me—that she will discover who she is and love herself completely.

How do girls discover who they are? Researchers have found that girls need to know we respect them, have high expectations for them, and, no matter what, love them. Most of all, they need to be heard. The girl who has adults who listen to her is likely to grow up strong. How wonderful that we can provide what our daughters need most—a listening ear backed by a listening heart.

That's why the editors of American Girl have gathered letters from girls who could be my daughters or yours. Full of opinion, wonder, and sometimes pain, the letters remind us to listen. So do the e-mail responses from older girls gathered through our partner on this project, SmartGirl.com. Together, these voices give us a good idea of what's on the minds of all kinds of American girls.

Finally, you'll also find in these pages insight and advice from the best experts in the field. Experienced therapists and educators, many of whom have contributed to *Daughters*, provide background on what girls are going through and caring advice on what you can do when your daughter is in similar situations. These are writers who know what it takes to be a parent and who remember what it took to be a girl—writers who remind us to remember who we are.

All the best to you and your daughters.

Editor, *Daughters*™ Newsletter

"Listen to Me!"

by Evelyn Bassoff, Ph.D.

> *"I can't tell my parents anything. Whether I'm upset, sad, or mad, I can't talk. My dad never understands and just complains, 'What a stupid thing to worry about.' If I tell my mom, she doesn't really get it and ends up telling my dad. I can't trust anyone."*
> Age 14

In your daughter's early years, she accepts without question your wisdom and authority, idealizing you as a superior being. As she enters her preteen years, though, you may notice that your golden crown begins to tarnish. Becoming aware that you are merely human and fallible, she begins to challenge your views and lets you know that everything you do—the way you dress, eat, talk, clear your throat, and laugh—embarrasses her. As she works to develop an identity that is separate from yours, she's also apt to be less open, to keep secrets, or even to lie.

As she moves into adolescence, your daughter's communications with you may worsen. There may be times when she is irritable and impatient with you (most notably when she is unhappy with herself), and you may be alternately angry,

> *"My mother and I fight all the time. We love each other one hour, and the next we hate each other! I really hate fighting with her, but I don't like doing anything that other people want me to do."*
> age 14

hurt, or just plain worn out as a result of the tension. Sometimes, it's hard to believe that she still needs and loves you. But the truth is that she does—very much.

Learning to Listen

One of the biggest frustrations you may find as a parent is that communication between you and your daughter closes down at the very time you feel an urgency to prepare her for the world outside her home. You have so much good advice to impart and experience from which she would benefit, but all too often when you try to talk to her, she rolls her eyes and walks away, leaving you dangling in mid-sentence.

It came as a big shock to me when my daughter, who as a little girl had mimicked and emulated me, was no longer interested in my "pearls of wisdom." Leah was about 12 years old when I initiated a discussion about sex. Because my own mother had avoided telling me the facts of life, I stumbled through adolescence hopelessly misinformed and was determined not to let this happen to Leah. However, minutes after I began my little discourse, Leah's eyes glazed over, and she blithely informed me that she already knew everything there was to know. That was the end of that.

Gradually, I began to figure out two things. The first was that as she separated from me, she would find other people—Dad, teachers, coaches, Grandma, and mothers of friends—to be her mentors. I didn't have to do it all. The second was that

> *"The best thing about my mom is that she can sense how I'm feeling. If I'm crabby, she gives me space. If I'm upset, we talk. It's like she's my diary that gives advice and a shoulder to cry on."*
> *age 11*

she would need my sympathetic ear more than my advice. At this stage in her life, I had to learn how to become a good listener and be available when she wanted to talk. My initiating heart-to-hearts—as I found out many times—only pushed her away.

Understanding Equals Respect

The letter that introduces this chapter speaks of an adolescent girl's strong desire to be listened to and understood. This 14-year-old girl wants her parents to respect her feelings instead of trivializing them, as her father does, or betraying her confidences, as her mother does.

Often when we parents minimize our daughters' travails, our intention is to help our daughters distinguish between the mountain and the molehill. However, if you do this, your daughter is likely to interpret it as disrespect or total lack of understanding. The father of our letter writer would show his daughter that he took her seriously if he said something like, "You're obviously feeling very upset (or mad or sad). If you want to talk, I'll be glad to listen." And before her mother revealed her daughter's confidences, she might say something to this effect: "Both your dad and I care how you're feeling. We often talk about ways we can be helpful to you. Is it okay with you if I tell him what you've shared with me?"

It's not easy to be a good listener. It requires you to be interested in your daughter's ideas, willing to listen to her without judgment, and prepared to let her change your mind. That can feel risky, because you may think that as the parent, what you say goes. If you really want your daughter to talk to you, you also need to give her your undivided attention, which may mean turning off the TV, not answering the ringing phone, and shutting down the computer. Making eye contact also tells her, "Yes, I'm here. I'm paying attention to you."

Being a good listener also means restraining yourself from interrupting, contradicting, debating, or launching into a discussion about yourself when your daughter is talking. Your object should be not to score points but to understand. Good listening doesn't mean you have to sit in silence with an approving grin as she chatters on. You ought to be asking questions— not for the purpose of giving her the third degree, but to clarify. "I'm not

> *"I love talking to my mom. She always listens to me and doesn't interrupt. I can talk to her about anything, and she will always give me positive advice. I feel very confident after I talk to her."*
> Age 11

sure I understand," you might say. "Could you give me another example or say it in another way?" Check to make sure that you're on track: "It sounds to me as if you're saying _____. Am I right? If I'm not—if I'm misunderstanding you—please tell me what I'm getting wrong."

When She Says Things You'd Rather Not Hear

Of course, it's a pleasure to listen to your daughter when she shares parts of herself that make you proud or make you laugh.

> *"Whenever I try to tell my parents something I'm mad about, they always take the other side. I like to tell my mom things because I want us to be close, but I don't think I can do it if she always takes the other side."*
> Age 12

You are put to the test when she attacks your beliefs, asserts her differences, or tells you how unhappy she is. It may not be easy to hear "Dad, I know you think my being on the basketball team is the greatest thing that ever happened to me, but I've decided to quit" or "Mom, you may believe in God, but I don't." It's less easy to keep your emotions in check when she says, "I hate it that you got divorced, and I'm totally not interested in meeting your new friend," or worst of all, "Don't you understand that I hate my life and don't want to live anymore?"

If you overreact when your daughter says things you'd rather not hear, you will shut her down. During these difficult conversations, she is asking herself, "Can my mom and dad accept me and love me even if I'm not living my life to please them?" Internally, she may be feeling, "Are Mom and Dad strong enough to be there for me when I'm in trouble, or will I end up taking care of them because they're so upset about me?"

If you really want your daughter to talk about what is going on in her life, learn to stay as calm as possible when she opens up. Help reduce her anxiety by putting things in perspective for her: "Yes, today everything went wrong, but you can make a fresh start tomorrow." Help her figure out options by prompting, "What are your choices here?" Remind her we all make mistakes with something like, "I guess that like the rest of us, you're not perfect." Assure her that the emotional pain she's suffering now is not permanent by suggesting, "The one thing we can be sure of is change."

> *"I can't tell my mom about my problems because then she gets really depressed."*
> Age 11

Just as you can soothe your daughter when she is in a crisis, you can soothe yourself by calling on your gentle or lighthearted inner voice. Remind yourself that this too shall pass. When you're anxious, tell yourself, "It's all right. Take a deep breath," and "Whoever said that raising a teenage girl would be easy?"

When your daughter is in crisis, you need to be especially careful to nurture yourself both physically and emotionally—physically by getting ample sleep, exercise, and good nutrition, and emotionally by sharing your heartaches with trusted souls and finding spiritual solace. It behooves you not to fall apart when your daughter does because she needs you to be the strong support who will help her get through her bad times. If her troubles are too big to handle alone, get professional help for her and/or for yourself.

Understanding Boundaries

The fact that you are willing to listen to your daughter doesn't necessarily mean you will agree with her. After fully understanding why it is so important for your 14-year-old to party with her friends on a school night, you may still think it's a bad idea and not allow it. During the preteen and teen years, your daughter absolutely needs limits and boundaries. When she pushes you to agree to something that in your gut you know is unreasonable or dangerous, you must say, "No, I won't permit this. It goes against my best judgment."

"My parents treat me like I'm five years old. All my friends can see PG-13 movies, and my dad doesn't even let me see plain PG movies. I feel embarrassed around my friends."
Age 10

All too often, we parents back down because we are afraid that if we set and enforce limits, our daughters will hate us, blow up, or run away. If, as children, we were physically or verbally abused, we may be fearful of repeating abusive patterns with our own children and worry unnecessarily that any frustration we express will explode into a rage. With that in mind, we may avoid conflicts at any cost. However, setting and enforcing limits are essential to good parenting. Research tells us that adolescents grow up to be socially responsible, independent, and self-confident when parents are both affectionate and strict—when we are clear with our children that the love we have for them can't be shaken, yet we are also not overly permissive or indulgent with their needs.

One of the differences between younger and older girls is that younger girls often do well with clear, consistent rules, while older girls resist and defy them. Although giving in to an older adolescent's unreasonable demands is never in her best interest, the "Do it because I say so" approach can backfire. Instead of laying down hard-and-fast rules, negotiate with your daughter toward an acceptable compromise. By negotiating with her, you show her that you take her ideas seriously and that she has the power to influence you if her arguments are persuasive.

Chances are, however, that no matter what rational boundaries you set for your daughter, there will come a time when she defies them. She may go someplace with her friends after you told her not to, or she may lie about who she's been with or how she spent an evening. Some amount of deception is to be expected in adolescence. Your daughter might lie because she needs privacy or because she wants to try something new and she feels you are too restrictive. She takes a risk as an attempt to get more freedom and move toward independence.

Of course, as parents we place restrictions on our daughters' behaviors for their own protection, but they don't always see that. The best we can do is try to give girls as much freedom as they can handle *safely*. If your daughter deceives you, enforce whatever consequences your family has set up. Let her know that her safety is your primary concern. Take heart—usually, as they mature, girls become more sure of themselves and have less need to lie.

Trust Her and She'll Trust Herself

Your daughter may act as though she couldn't care less about your opinions of her, but the truth is, she cares a great deal. If she has lied to you in the past, she'll have to work to regain your confidence by being honest. It's only when you trust her that she can trust herself. If you don't trust her, she can't help believing that she'll mess up. That's why the bottom line of so many arguments is "Why can't you just trust me!"

Of course, your biggest wish is probably no different from hers: you want to trust your daughter. More than anything, you want to trust that the moment-to-moment decisions she makes will keep her safe and sound. If you take every opportunity to validate her when she shows good judgment, acts responsibly, thinks things through, handles crises, copes with hardship, or demonstrates adaptability, you reinforce her trustworthiness.

It's also important to give your daughter opportunities to expand her capabilities and increase her life skills, which could mean getting a summer job, participating in a wilderness program, doing community work, or learning how to drive. If you know your daughter well, you'll have a pretty good idea of what she can handle. Encourage her to try new things and to venture out into the world. The sweetest words to her ear will be "You can do this. I have confidence in you."

Dr. Evelyn Bassoff is a practicing psychologist, a mother, and the author of several parenting books, including **Mothers and Daughters: Loving and Letting Go** *and* **Cherishing Our Daughters: How Parents Can Raise Girls to Become Confident Women.** *For seven years, she was the "Marriage and Sex" columnist for* **Parents** *magazine.*

LISTENING IN

Girls open up about trust, discussing hard subjects, and fighting with their parents. Dr. Bassoff shares insight on what to do when your daughter has similar fears.

"You just don't get it."

"It's hard to talk to my parents because they don't understand that things they are trying to tell me now are things I learned when I was 10. They don't see that teenagers these days are much more mature than when they were growing up."
Age 13

Dr. Bassoff: The girl who wrote this letter makes a good point. Girls today are growing up faster than we did—probably by three to four years. In our era, there was no MTV, Internet, or tragedy at Columbine High School. However, the fact that our daughters are pressured to act and look older than their years does not make them more emotionally mature than we were at their age.

No matter how worldly your adolescent daughter may seem, she still needs your guidance and limit setting. If she balks at restrictions, it can help to remind her that privileges and responsibilities will increase as she gets older: "Now you're old enough to baby-sit. Next year, you can go to the mall without us and shop for clothes with your friends."

The next time she insists on being treated like a full adult, say to her, "It's true that you know a lot more about sex, drugs, violence—and a whole bunch of other things—than we did at your age. You're also under more pressure to be sophisticated than we were at age 13. Our job as parents is to see that you don't get into situations that are over your head." As much as she may grumble about being treated like a kid (which, after all, is what she really is), she will also secretly feel relief at not being hurried into adulthood and at having parents who protect her childhood.

"All my friends think my mom is cool, but it bugs me when she tells jokes. Sometimes they're funny, but she acts like my friend and not my mom, and most of the time I don't like that."
Age 12

Dr. Bassoff: This girl wants her mom to be her mom, not one of her friends. My hunch is that she also doesn't want her mom to compete for her friends' attention, which is what happens when Mom entertains them with her jokes. The best thing this girl's mom could do the next time her daughter's friends are over is to greet them warmly, then leave the girls to themselves.

In our youth-idealizing culture, some of us find it hard to let go of our younger selves. (After all, we are of the generation that couldn't trust anyone over 30.) You may believe that in order to have a close relationship with your daughter, you need to be her buddy. Not so. You can be a fun-loving parent with strong ties to your daughter while respecting the boundaries that separate you from her and her peers. Just as you encourage your daughter to behave in an age-appropriate way, you also need to be age-appropriate—in the way you dress, joke around, and generally conduct yourself. If you act younger than your years, your daughter won't trust that she can turn to you as a guide.

"Some things are hard to say."
"I can tell my mom anything, ask her anything, and never worry about being criticized. If I'm nervous about talking to her about something, I like to write her a letter about it. It's much less stressful. And I love to read the things she writes."
Age 12

Dr. Bassoff: Writing letters is surely one of the finest ways to communicate. Unlike conversation, which moves along so swiftly, writing slows us down. When we write, we are able to order and clarify our thoughts. No one interrupts us. We can take as long as we want to frame our ideas, to start and stop at will. And, as this 12-year-old explains, letter writing is a way of sharing what may be too embarrassing to say face-to-face. Even a daughter with a warm, nonjudgmental mother will, at times, find it hard to bring up the personal problems and worries that the teen years are famous for.

By writing letters to each other, this mother-daughter pair has come upon a splendid way to communicate. Why not follow their lead? The next time you want to get your daughter something special, consider buying her a packet of lovely notepaper. Suggest that when she has concerns (large or small) that she feels awkward discussing, she can choose to write to you about them, and you'll respond with a short note of your own.

"I'm having a problem right now. I don't know how to talk to my mom about puberty. I know she would help me, but I don't know where to start."
Age unknown

Dr. Bassoff: This girl needs a little coaching so that it will be easier for her to open up and ask the questions that are troubling her. A caution to dads: As you know, your involvement with your adolescent daughter is important to her in countless ways, but tread lightly around discussing her emerging sexual feelings and the details of her changing body. Dads can reinforce their daughters' positive feelings about their physical selves by giving compliments that are general but loving. Be sure to say, simply, "You look fantastic today," or "You are growing up to be a beautiful young woman."

Dad can also give his daughter a much-needed male perspective on what adolescent boys are experiencing—did Dad feel gawky and gangly when he was 12 years old?

Might the boy who is calling to ask her out be as nervous as she is? That can be reassuring for girls to hear.

For mothers, disclosing personal information is a way to break the ice. You might say, "When I was in puberty, I worried about popping my pimples— would I scar my skin? I felt stupid because I didn't know how to use a tampon. I wondered if it was bad to masturbate. Puberty is worry time! So, honey, when you have questions or worries, just whisper in my ear, 'Mom, can we have a couple of minutes to talk?' Or you can even write me a note if that's less embarrassing. I promise I'll keep what you say confidential."

One way to encourage an adolescent to bring up personal matters is to set up a regular "date"—say once or twice a month—for getting together and talking. That's not to say a mom shouldn't talk about sex or periods or zits with her daughter while they're doing the dishes together or driving to school. The only necessary conditions for a heart-to-heart are privacy and the daughter's willingness to talk.

"Let me be!"

"Some of my problems I want to talk out with another person, but others I want to work through myself. When I'm working them out on my own, I usually look sad, which makes my mom start bugging me. She says, 'Tell me! Tell me!' The more I say I don't want to talk about it, the worse she gets."
Age 12

Dr. Bassoff: This girl is sending her mom important messages: "Let me grow up and try to work things out for myself. Please don't get bent out of shape if I'm not always happy. Let me wrestle with the hard things. If I discover that I'm in over my head, I'll ask for help." Her desire to figure things out for herself is a sign of her healthy development. My guess is that her mom wants to remove all the stones from her daughter's path. She can't, of course, which is a good thing. When we jump in with both feet to fix every problem our children encounter, we deprive them of the opportunities to become resourceful.

This mom may believe it is unhealthy for her daughter to keep anything to herself—or it may just be in Mom's nature to push her daughter to talk. Whereas extro-verted people like to talk things out, introverted people are more private and look inward to process their thoughts, feelings, and emotions. If you find yourself in a situation in which your daughter says, "I don't want to talk about it," try to say, "No problem, honey," and walk away. Ralph Waldo Emerson put it this way: "Respect the child. Be not too much his parent. Trespass not on his solitude."

"Stop treating me like a baby."

"My parents are so protective that I can't stand it. They won't let me go to parties if a boy is going, too. They want to get background checks on my friends! I want them to trust me and my friends."
Age unknown

Dr. Bassoff: It seems these parents have decided they will do everything necessary to keep their daughter safe, including forbidding her to interact with boys and anyone else who could potentially do her harm. The problem is that these overly strict rules imprison this girl and deprive her of the joy of being a teenager. If she is made to believe it is unsafe for her to go anywhere with anyone, she is also likely to develop excessive fears about people and places.

We need to remember that our primary roles are to prepare our youngsters to venture out into the world with enthusiasm and optimism and to teach them to deal with the ups and downs they'll inevitably encounter. You can give your daughter guidelines and good counsel. You can also set conditions, such as "You can't go out on a school night," "You need to be home by midnight," or "When you get to your friend's house, you need to give us a call." You can even encourage your daughter to enroll in self-defense classes.

However, it is not right to keep your daughter under lock and key. The paradox is that children who are overprotected grow up to be very vulnerable to real-life dangers because they don't get the chance to learn the survival skills that are their real protection. Also, once they are emancipated, they may go hog-wild and end up in the kind of trouble their parents tried desperately to prevent.

When parents are deeply mistrustful or afraid, it is important that they get help from a mental-health professional. They may be suffering from an anxiety disorder, which not only disrupts a parent's life but can promote anxiety in a child as well.

"My mom won't let me and my sisters watch anything but educational TV, and we're not babies. I'm very, very angry. My sisters and I do a lot of other things to educate ourselves: we play piano and sports, we get good grades, and my sister is starring in her school play. I've tried talking to my mom, but she won't see reason."
Age 11

Dr. Bassoff: Adolescents naturally push against the limits we parents set for them, just as this 11-year-old is doing. Sometimes our saying "No" will make them very angry. They'll rant and rave, roll their eyes, and try to convince us that we're unreasonable. This is especially true when we don't let them do something that their peers get to do. But we need to remember that their anger at our rules is a normal part of their growing up—not cause for us to cave in to their demands. Our job as parents is to use our best judgment in setting and enforcing rules that reinforce our family values, which is what this mom is doing.

However, the tensions between this girl and her mom might ease up if Mom respectfully listened to her daughter's point of view and conveyed that she understood her distress. "You have good reasons for wanting more TV freedom," she might say, "but I have to do what I think is right as your mom." It's also possible that as she listens with an open mind to her daughter's grievances, she'll find a way to bend her rule somewhat without compromising her principles as a parent.

"My mom doesn't trust me enough to let me walk around the mall with friends or do just about anything. Of course, she always gets her way. But she doesn't know that I sneak out."
Age 13

Dr. Bassoff: Every girl will from time to time go against her parents' wishes. Telling an occasional lie or "sneaking out" once in a while are pretty typical teenage behaviors. But if the defiance becomes a pattern, there may be a disconnection in family relationships that needs fixing.

When your daughter doesn't feel that you trust her, she is more likely to act out on a regular basis.

"If my parents don't believe me anyway, even when I'm being good, I might as well be bad," she may tell herself. Perhaps you have very good reasons for the restrictions you set. However, it would really help your relationship and your daughter's self-esteem if you could let her know that it's the situation, not her, that you don't trust. "I know you're a good kid," you might say, "but the mall isn't an appropriate place for a young girl to hang out."

There's no way of telling from this short letter if this mom is being too restrictive. My hunch is that this young girl's claim that she won't let her "do just about anything" is an exaggeration. However, if Mom's rules are truly unreasonable, then she needs to take stock. When we imprison our children with overly strict rules, we can expect that they'll rebel.

"Can't we stop fighting?"

"I argue with my mom all the time. I feel like I have to prove myself to her, even though I really know I don't. Her feelings often get hurt, and that makes me feel bad. I wish I could stop wanting to argue."
Age 13

Dr. Bassoff: This girl just can't help getting angry and defiant with her parents. Young teenagers are often irritable and impatient. They are up against so many pressures at school and with peers that they are apt to take out their frustrations on the people they know will love them no matter what—their parents. As much as your young teen rants, "Stop treating me like a baby!" growing up is threatening to her, and she is secretly angry with you because she can't allow your babying anymore.

This girl writes, "I feel like I have to prove myself to her, even though I really know I don't." In other words, she has to prove to herself that she is tough enough to take on the world, and she tries to do this by standing up to her parent. On top of all the psychological turmoil, add in the mood swings caused by hormonal changes, and you might better understand the volatility she feels!

In a household with a young teen, can you stop all the fighting? Probably not. However, you can calm things down. When your daughter is grumpy, a comment from you like "You seem troubled. Do you want to talk?" can abort an angry outburst. So can a mutual time-out. "Let's face it," we can say, "this conversation is no picnic for either of us. Why don't we give each other a little space before things get out of hand and we really hurt each other's feelings."

The girl who wrote this letter doesn't like being mean. When your daughter acts this way, in fact, hurting you makes her feel very guilty. By setting and enforcing rules for fighting fairly, you can prevent her from stepping over the lines. These rules needn't be complicated: no interrupting, name-calling, profanity, degrading remarks, or yelling. At the first infraction, look her in the eye and let her know that you take it seriously and that it's absolutely not acceptable. In spite of her reaction, your daughter probably wants to act respectfully. Your job is to help her accomplish this.

"When you think I can't stand you, remember this . . ."

When your daughter is angry or resisting you, it may feel as if you are her least favorite person in the world. There's no denying that rejection hurts. When you feel as if she has lost all respect for you, remember: her anger is temporary but her admiration for you is not.

"My mom and I fight half the time, but usually she's really funny and cool to hang out with."
Age 11

"My dad is really positive about things. He can always make me laugh when times are the worst."
Age 13

"I love my mom. She's the best! I admire how she can just keep on going and striving for the best, even if there are tough obstacles in the way."
Age 12

"My father grew up in a bad town, and I admire him for not allowing himself to be poisoned by all the stuff in that town."
Age 12

"I admire that my mom does handiwork and fixes things around the house. It shows that girls can do that stuff, too."
Age 10

"I like that my mom has her own ideas and doesn't let people walk all over her."
Age 11

"My father is always there to cheer me up. When I am with him, I feel so happy."
Age 14

"What I like best about my relationship with my mom is the times we go into the kitchen and cook. It gives us time to talk. With my dad, I like working in the shop. I inherited his sense of humor, and sometimes we laugh so hard we can't work."
Age 11

YOUR ROLE

Know her world. Encourage her to open up by making efforts to know who she is. Show interest in her creative work. Listen to her favorite CDs or movies with her.

Listen and validate. Even if you don't agree with her, be willing to see her point of view. You might say, "Yes, I can see that having an earlier curfew than your friends makes you feel babyish."

Require respect. If a discussion turns nasty with yelling or name-calling, stop the talk immediately. Say, "I'm calling a time-out. We'll continue later when we can show each other some respect."

Follow your instincts. If she asks permission to do something you are really uncomfortable with, listen to your gut—no matter how much she insists you're more unreasonable than other adults.

Give yourself time to think. If you're not sure how to respond to a request, say, "I can't give an answer yet. I need to think it over."

Stick to the point. When you give feedback, be brief and specific. For example, "I'd appreciate it if you stopped rolling your eyes when I ask you to help with housework."

Accentuate the positive. The surest way to increase your daughter's trustworthiness is to express your approval when she acts with good judgment and thinks things through clearly.

Get to know her friends' parents. Arrange a potluck dinner for her friends and their folks. Agree to call one another as needed—to check on the whereabouts of a daughter or share other concerns.

Lean on a friend. When the responsibilities, worries, or hurt feelings that come with being a parent get you down, vent your frustrations with a trusted friend, family member, or therapist.

Her Changing Body

by Lynda Madison, Ph.D.

"My body is changing. I'm growing in some places but staying the same in others. My attitude is changing, too. One minute I'm happy and the next I'm the saddest person on earth. My mom says I'm going through puberty. I'm just 10 years old, for crying out loud! That's supposed to happen to 12- and 13-year-olds, right? Is it okay to be embarrassed to talk to Mom about all of this?"

Age 10

Your daughter's growing up! Both you and she have noticed. And like you, your daughter has feelings of both excitement and fear about that fact. The young writer above describes the mixed feelings many girls have as they enter puberty. She is puzzled by the changes in her body, confused by her emotions, and unsure how to talk about her feelings. Because hormonal changes can start months before any outward physical signs, fluctuating emotions can be the first signal that a girl is entering puberty.

Hormones can contribute to your daughter's moodiness during her preteen years, but anxiety and uncertainty play big roles, too. Parents are often dismayed by their daughter's angry words, demands to be left alone, and melodramatic expressiveness. Withdrawal and rudeness are not signs that your daughter is shutting you out. More likely, she is vacillating between wanting to be older and wishing she could stay secure as your little girl. Do not let your anger, disappointment, or resentment of her moodiness weaken the communication you have with her. Setting boundaries and consequences for her is important, but so is gentle reassurance that her experiences are normal and that you are not going to abandon her just because she is growing up. The first steps you can take are to encourage her to talk to you, show her that you are willing to discuss any topic she brings up, and have factual information so you can give her accurate answers.

Puberty Is Not a Race

When your daughter compares her development to her friends', puberty may feel like a competition. Who is developing first? Who has started her period? Clearly girls develop at different rates, but they all go through the same general stages. Somewhere between the ages of 8 and 13, a girl's brain releases a chemical called gonadotropin-releasing hormone, or GnRH, which signals her body to begin to mature. Often, a girl's hands, legs, and feet grow first, which can cause some awkwardness as she gets used to these changes. Most girls experience a growth spurt during puberty, during which they grow rapidly for a period of two to three years. About the time this growth spurt begins, a girl's breasts and pubic hair will begin to develop. Physicians sometimes break down puberty into specific stages of breast and pubic-hair growth. (See "The Stages of Physical Development," page 23.)

> "My breasts are growing, I'm getting hair under my armpits, and I'm scared of what else might happen. I keep bumping into walls because I'm growing. I feel rushed, like I have not had enough time to be a kid."
> Age 10

The Stages of Physical Development

The books that your daughter reads about puberty may break the adolescent growth process down into five stages. Knowing these stages can help you better relate to her thoughts and concerns.

Stage One: Before Puberty. The breast area and nipples are level with the chest. The circle around the nipple, the *areola,* is small and light. No pubic hair is present.

Stage Two: Early Puberty. The breast and nipple rise up in a small mound that some call a *breast bud.* The circle of the areola gets larger and often darker in color. Soft, fine hair (usually light-colored and straight) grows in the center of the pubic area.

Stage Three: Middle Puberty. This stage usually begins a few months to a year after Stage Two starts. The breast and areola get larger, the areola gets darker, and the breasts become pointier. More pubic hair grows, and it is darker and beginning to curl.

Stage Four: Late Puberty. The areola and nipple rise above the level of the breast to form a separate curve. The pubic hair becomes coarse and curly. It now covers more of the pubic area but less than an adult's hair will.

Stage Five: Adulthood. The breast is mature, having a fuller and rounder appearance. The nipple sticks out. The areola is level with the rest of the breast. Pubic hair forms the shape of an upside-down triangle and spreads to the thighs.

Many physicians believe girls today are developing much younger than they were just a decade or two ago. Although 12 is the average age for a girl to begin her period, it is not uncommon for girls to start developing breasts and pubic hair when they are as young as 8 or 9 years old. Some scientists think this is due to obesity, whereas others blame it on chemicals in the environment or hormones in the meat we eat. Research shows that Hispanic, African American, and Asian/Pacific Island girls may begin menstruating earlier than Caucasian girls.[1] Talk to your daughter's physician if you are concerned that your daughter is an "early bloomer."

Getting Her Period

Your daughter will probably start menstruating about six months to two years after she shows the first changes of puberty: a growth spurt, breast development, or pubic hair. If your daughter asks for a technical explanation of what menstruation is all about, you may want to brush up on your facts. (See "The Facts—Period," at right.)

During puberty, your daughter will grow in stages. There will probably be a time when

1. C. Koprowski et al., "Diet, Body Size and Menarche in a Multiethnic Cohort," *British Journal of Cancer* 79 (April 1999): 1907–11.

The Facts—Period

A refresher on what happens when a girl gets her period.

Step One: The brain hormone GnRH travels to the pituitary gland, which releases *lutenizing hormone* (LH) and *follicle-stimulating hormone* (FSH).

Step Two: These hormones go to the ovaries, which begin producing the hormone *estrogen.* Estrogen, LH, and FSH work together to prepare a girl's body for the possibility of pregnancy.

Step Three: One of a girl's two ovaries releases one of the several thousand eggs her body has carried since birth. As the egg travels through the fallopian tube to the uterus, the uterus builds up a lining of extra blood and tissue. If the egg were to be fertilized, the lining would feed and protect a developing baby.

Step Four: When no pregnancy occurs, the extra blood and tissue are shed through the vagina as a menstrual period. Periods happen about every 28 days.

she widens around the waist and hips before she gains an inch or two in height. Girls need about 17 percent body fat in order to develop and begin their periods, so weight gain during this time is normal and necessary. Even gaining up to 25 pounds during a growth spurt in puberty can be perfectly normal. If your daughter is struggling with excess weight gain, be careful not to discourage or tease her about this sensitive topic. Talk discreetly to her doctor, and then approach the issue as a need for healthier eating and exercise rather than placing undue attention on her physical appearance and dieting.

The Brain Gain

Your daughter's body is not the only thing growing like wildfire during her preteen years: her brain is also developing rapidly and in increasingly complex ways. At this stage, your daughter will develop more sophisticated math skills, become more verbally expressive, and learn to generate hypotheses in science. These newly formed skills also translate to her way of looking at the world and her relationships with others. She practices hypothesis testing with parents and friends ("Can I get away with this?" "Does he like me or not?"). She spends more time thinking about things like friendships and religion, and as she progresses into the teen years, her introspection will allow her to question her place in the world.

As your daughter becomes able to think more deeply about possibilities and choices, she may become self-conscious about the opinions she believes others are forming of her. Ironically, in spite of her growing ability to think more analytically, she will sometimes jump to conclusions rather than stopping to consider alternatives. She may develop a sense that there is a "universal audience" out there, one in which everyone is looking at her or judging her in some way. This can make her touchy and easily upset by even the most benign comments and actions.

The Social Side of Physical Changes

Because girls develop physically at very different rates, some will look like high schoolers while others show no signs of puberty at all. This can be difficult if your daughter falls at either extreme. If she is slow to develop, she might feel embarrassed and insecure. She will need your reassurance that she will probably catch up to her peers and that there are other important areas, such as academics and sports, on which to focus her attention while she waits. If women in

> *"My chest is completely flat. In the locker room at school, all the girls— even my friends—make fun of me. They say I'm immature and look like I belong in kindergarten. I am too embarrassed to talk to my mom about it."*
> age 14

your family are naturally small-busted, you may expect that your daughter will be, too. Point out the good things that go along with having smaller breasts, such as freedom of movement and ease of exercise. Or think of a female family member that your daughter admires who has a similar body type; point out how breast size has not stopped this relative from being a fun-loving, likable person.

Early developers often are subjected to teasing and face pressures that others do not experience until they are older. Sadly, more than two-thirds of all eighth graders experience unwelcome sexual advances, which can range from taunting comments to being pressed up against a locker and groped.[2] Girls who have been harassed often tend to be fearful in school and lack confidence in

2. "Hostile Hallways: The AAUW Survey on Sexual Harassment in America's Schools" (American Association of University Women, 1993).

themselves. Your daughter will need to be ready for this type of stress. Talk with her about how to handle unwelcome sexual attention and how to stay safe. Give her words to say like, "Stop it! I don't like that," and "I said 'No.' " Suggest several adults at her school to whom she can turn if she ever feels uneasy.

During her middle-school years, your daughter has an increasing need for support, advice, and sharing, which she fulfills primarily through friendships with other girls. But friendships are fluid at this age, as girls try out new roles and new ways to feel accepted. Only around 20 percent of girls name the same best friend from one year to the next. If your daughter decides her looks are the key to her popularity, she risks feeling that to maintain her self-worth she must behave or dress provocatively or start dating early. If she does these things, she will leave her peer group behind and miss out on much of the support she would receive from other girls. Help your daughter develop a variety of skills, qualities, and activities so that her self-esteem and identity are not defined by just her physical appearance. Prove that you value her, too, and not just for how she looks but also for who she is and how she thinks, acts, and treats other people.

"I am playing on two softball teams right now. I have decided to become very dedicated to the sport. I am proud that I am strong enough to do it and that I never give up."
Age 14

This sense of diversifying also applies to your daughter's comfort with her body. Give her many ways to learn physical control and awareness, such as through sports, music, or dancing. By becoming more aware of her body's position in space and by learning to enjoy movement and activity, she will build her self-confidence. Compliment her abilities, and let her know you are impressed with her efforts. She will need lots of encouragement to offset the temptation to take shortcuts to popularity and self-improvement.

She Really Needs You

A girl whose changing body seems different and awkward and who is receiving conflicting messages from friends, magazines, movies, and television can feel confused and frightened about what it is like to grow up and what will be expected of her when she does. Your best gift to your daughter is your willingness to discuss what is going on.

Mothers, your daughter will watch you closely for clues about how to act and feel about being a woman. So talk to her! Do not expect her to bring up personal issues if you do not model talking about feelings. Show a willingness to discuss all sorts of topics, both physical and emotional. She can easily give the impression that she is more "together" and mature than she really is. Do not assume she does not need information from you.

Fathers, you can be especially helpful to your daughter. You can talk about what young boys are like and how valuable a girl's self-respect is. You can help steer her focus to things other than physical appearance and boys. You can help her think for herself and analyze what she sees. Remember that if you don't point out the inappropriateness of demeaning messages about women or sexually explicit material in popular culture, she is likely to believe that you approve and agree.

Both parents, but especially mothers, can talk about the slang words your daughter hears and give her proper terms for body parts and sexual intercourse. Your daughter will need guidance to become responsible for what she does with her body. Of course, she will not turn to you with every question, and that's okay, too.

Girls need privacy, time to think things over, and intimate chats with friends. But you will want your daughter to know that *you* know what's going on in the world, that you have accurate information about development and sexuality, and that you would love to talk to her if she ever has a question or concern.

Dr. Lynda Madison is the director of psychological services at Children's Hospital in Omaha, Nebraska. She is a practicing psychologist and author of **Keep Talking: A Mother-Daughter Guide to the Preteen Years** *and* **Parenting with Purpose.** *She has two daughters, ages 13 and 16.*

LISTENING IN

Girls open up with real-life concerns about what they see in the mirror, and Dr. Madison shares insight and advice on what to do when your daughter has similar fears.

"I need to talk to someone!"

"I feel like I'm starting puberty already. My mom said I wasn't, but while I was in the shower I noticed that my breasts were already in Stage Two. I want to tell my mom, but I'm too embarrassed because my dad and two brothers are always in the house. My mom is kind of stressed because we're moving. There's one other lady I really trust, but she would probably tell my mom anyway. I don't know if any other girl feels like I do."

Age 8

Dr. Madison: A busy lifestyle and a house full of people can work against a parent's efforts to be seen as available and willing to talk about puberty. This young girl is hungry for a private talk with her mother, which could reduce her concerns and help her feel excited rather than embarrassed about the changes in her body. Be sure to give your daughter plenty of opportunities to catch you alone and quiet, even if it means making a special date to spend time together. Also let her know that the conversations you have will remain confidential. If she cannot or does not talk to you, let her know she can talk to her doctor, the school nurse, or a counselor.

"I'm going to start middle school this year, and I can't stand the idea of having to take showers and change clothes in front of other girls in gym class. I know everyone's too busy trying to hide her own body to pay much attention to someone else's, but I'm very shy. Did I mention that there are no curtains on the showers?"

Age 11

Dr. Madison: It is unfortunate that gym class puts girls in the uncomfortable position of being naked in front of each other, just when self-consciousness is at its peak. However, one of the benefits of this kind of openness is that girls can see that there are many different body types and sizes.

If your daughter expresses these common fears, remind her that modesty is important but that her body is not something to be ashamed of, either. Encourage her to act confident and unconcerned in the locker room, even if she does not feel that way. Giving others power by hiding or getting stressed out will not help her problem. If other girls make unkind comments, help your daughter be ready to tell them that her body is none of their business and that she feels good about herself. If that does not solve things, she (or you) might need to talk to her teacher about other options for dressing and save her showers for home.

"I am so moody lately!"

"I've been feeling a wave of emotions lately that I can't control. Last week I felt very grouchy and angry for no reason. But this week I have been crying a lot, even when I'm not sad. I've never felt this way before, and it's scaring me."
Age 11

Dr. Madison: The ups and downs of your daughter's moods can make *both* of you feel as if you are on an emotional roller coaster. Hormones affect a girl physically, by making her tired or causing her breasts to be sore, and emotionally, by making her extra sensitive to situations that leave her happy, sad, angry, or upset. She might not even know exactly what emotion she is having, let alone why she is grumpy or crying.

Simply ask her if she is feeling angry or sad about something. Suggest that you are willing to listen to whatever she thinks might have prompted her feelings, and ask her what she thinks might happen next. There is nothing more frustrating than having a parent try to fix whatever is wrong before she or he fully understands the problem.

Sometimes simply hearing herself talk about the situation can help your daughter find a solution. Suggest she write about her feelings in a journal, or in a letter to herself or to you. By writing about what she was going through, she will need to clarify how she felt and what triggered her rush of emotions. Plus the feeling of getting those emotions out of her heart and onto a piece of paper can be cleansing.

Some children do develop depression during puberty, however, so be sure to seek the guidance of your physician or a psychologist if your daughter does not seem relieved by your repeated attempts to help.

"Most days I feel happy one minute and feel like crying the next. I get mad when people ask me about my day, and I always blow up at my mom. What is happening? Why do I do this?"
Age 10

Dr. Madison: This girl is describing the classic situation of "You always hurt the ones you love." Friendships can be tenuous and very important to young girls, but parents are safe people on whom to take out frustrations. After all, they are not going anywhere, and friends just might. If this girl understood that many girls go through the kinds of mood swings she's experiencing, she might be less distressed.

However, hormones cannot be blamed for everything and should not be used as an excuse for rude or inappropriate behavior. Even though a certain degree of acceptance of moodiness is in order, this girl will not feel secure or learn other ways of expressing her emotions if she is repeatedly allowed to be disrespectful of others. The timing must be right to discuss

sensitive feelings and emotional outbursts, and this is rarely in the throes of an argument. Get the message across that you care, and tell her you do not deserve to be treated rudely. Come back later to topics that are better discussed less heatedly, and give her other ways to say she is upset with whatever is bugging her.

"I'm worried about my period."
"What if my period starts when I'm in school and I have to tell the teacher? The boys might overhear and make fun of me. I'm really scared."
Age 10

Dr. Madison: The number-one concern of girls who have not yet started their periods is that they will be embarrassed in front of their peers. Knowing what is going to happen and being prepared with a plan can significantly reduce your daughter's worry and anxiety. Buy the napkins, tampons, or panty liners she will need before she starts her period and tell her how to use them. Show her where they will be kept, but also help her find a way to discreetly carry or store them at school in case she needs them. Reassure her that her teacher understands about periods and will respect her need for privacy, but let her know that if her period starts at school, she does not necessarily need to explain the details of what's happening at that very moment. She can simply ask to be excused to the restroom, then make a beeline to her locker or the nurse's office to get supplies.

Tips about tampons: There are no medical reasons young girls should shy away from tampons—comfort and responsibility are the key issues. Some girls as young as 11 or 12 use tampons easily, while other girls may find them uncomfortable. If your daughter is in the latter group but still wants to use tampons, have her try junior or slim-size products. Stress to any girl that she should change the tampon every four to six hours to avoid the risk of *toxic shock syndrome*, a rare but serious disease linked to prolonged tampon use. Be sure she uses the minimum absorbency that she needs to control her flow.

"My health teacher said that yellowish stuff in your underwear is a sign your period will come soon. Well, I have had that stuff in my underwear for at least four months, *and my period still hasn't come. Is something wrong with me?" Age 11*

Dr. Madison: Girls often notice a vaginal discharge several months before they start their periods, and they may be less alarmed if they know ahead of time that this can happen. This discharge cleanses the vaginal walls of old cells and most likely is normal if it is red, brown, clear, or milky white. However, a yellowish discharge, or one that has a bad odor to it, can be a sign of a yeast infection, caused by an overgrowth of the normal organisms in the moist vaginal area. Yeast infections are common and usually easy to clear up, but sometimes they cause itching or burning that can get pretty uncomfortable if not treated. Encourage your daughter to tell you if this happens. Consult her doctor if you think she has an infection or if over-the-counter medication does not clear it up. One way to help prevent yeast infections is for your daughter to wear cotton underwear that allows the area to get more air and stay drier.

"I started my period, and I don't like it. My mom tells me it's all a

part of growing up to be a woman.
I don't want to grow up! I am only
in the sixth grade, and I just want
to stay a girl. I don't know how to
talk to my mom about how I feel."
Age 11

**Dr. Madison: Some girls are very
bothered by their periods, and the
reasons for their dissatisfaction can
range from teasing, embarrassing
situations, fear of pregnancy, or
simply not liking the hassle. This
girl seems to fear that starting her
period means she is suddenly a different person, possibly one whom
her mother will reject as no longer
needing affection or comfort.
Ideally, her mother will notice her
anxiety, invite her to discuss her
feelings, and reassure her that she
is still going to be cherished and
cared for.**

**Your sensitivity will help your
daughter realize that starting
her period really does not change
things all that much. Menstruation
also may trigger fears in girls
who are having a particularly hard
time with the new pressures and
responsibilities of growing up. If
your openness and encouragement
do not help your daughter over
this hurdle, some professional
counseling may be needed.**

"Everyone's developing but me."
*"I still haven't started my period,
but all of my friends have. At my
friend's party, everyone was talking
about it, so I went away and
watched television. I feel weird
and really left out."*
Age 11

**Dr. Madison: Girls often become
concerned if they lag behind their
friends, especially because development is so often a part of their
conversation. If your daughter is in
a similar situation, remind her that
girls jump quickly from one activity
or topic to another, and she may
need only to wait for them to finish
this conversation. Leaving the
group, however, might make her
feel even more left out. By asking
questions and being open about
her menstrual status, your daughter might find her late start is not
as big a deal to her friends as it is
to her. You can also point out to
her that she will catch up with her
friends soon and that she will
know more about how to handle
things when she does, just from
hearing them talk.**

*"I am very discouraged, because
I am not as developed as my friends
are. It makes me feel like a baby! It
doesn't help that I'm also the third*

shortest girl in the class. All the boys like only the big-busted girls." Age 12

Dr. Madison: The changes your daughter will go through as she becomes a woman can make her feel very awkward at times. Our culture places a lot of emphasis on breasts, and so do girls (and, unfortunately, boys) during the preteen and teen years. Some girls worry that their breasts are not large enough and stuff their bras with tissues or wear padded bras to make up for it. These are not crimes, so be careful not to shame your daughter for doing them. Just assure her that she is attractive the way she is and that she does not need to be big-busted in order to be accepted. Although it might be hard for her to understand, let her know that other girls are unhappy because they think their breasts are too large, their nose is too long, or they are taller or shorter than they wish to be.

Some girls worry that one breast is developing before the other. If your daughter has that concern, let her know that this differential development is natural and that her breasts will probably even out once she reaches adulthood. Encourage her to talk to a nurse, doctor, or other adult friend if she needs more reassurance that she is developing normally.

"I don't know how to tell my parents that I need a bra."
"The only bra I have is a sports bra, and it rides up on me. I desperately want a regular bra, but I'm embarrassed and afraid to ask my mom. I don't really know which kind of bra I should have." Age 11

Dr. Madison: This girl is unsure that her parents have noticed the changes in her body and apparently does not feel free to talk to them about these concerns. Girls do not always know how to bring up difficult personal issues because they worry how their parents will respond. An astute parent might notice that this girl has developed beyond her sports bra, ask if she is comfortable, and suggest that they shop for something more appropriate, even if it is only a different style of sports bra. Some parents worry that giving a child a bra in the fourth or fifth grade is pushing her into growing up prematurely. Remember that some girls begin developing at eight or nine years of age and truly need a bra by the time they are 11. Keeping up with her peers in this way does not harm anyone.

"My chest is too big."

"I have a very big bust for my age. Everyone notices. All the boys ask me if my breasts are fake. The girls are either jealous or think I'm a slut and a tramp. It really bugs me. I cannot help it if my breasts are big! I need to know how to get people's attention off my chest."
Age 13

Dr. Madison: Some girls who develop early see their bust as something to be proud of, but most are a little bothered and need help dealing with unwelcome comments or advances.

If this is the situation with your daughter, remind her that other people cannot know her based just on her appearance. Teach her how to dress so as not to accentuate her bustline. Reassure her that this attention will ultimately pass and that she does not need to respond to every petty comment. Help her focus on her activities and skills so that she receives attention and a sense of achievement not based solely on her physical appearance. Finally, work out a plan for her to report any lewd

teasing or sexual advances to a sensitive teacher or counselor and, of course, to you.

"I *have* to shave my legs."

"I'm not allowed to shave my legs yet, because my mom says I'm too young. She says she didn't start shaving her legs until she was 14 years old! But all the girls in my school already shave. I have woolly mammoth legs, and I hate it."
Age 12

Dr. Madison: Although hair growth can vary, underarm hair usually starts to develop and leg hair darkens soon after pubic hair and breasts have begun to develop. Understand just how self-conscious your daughter can feel about this. Some parents are concerned that shaving at a young age is a sign that they are letting their daughter grow up too soon or that other adults will criticize their decision. Remember that girls today are developing earlier than in the past, and they see that shaving dark hair is something culturally acceptable for adults to do. Many girls still in elementary school begin shaving.

If you are not comfortable having your daughter remove the hair on her legs right now, be careful not to set an arbitrary age for shaving, particularly one based on when you began to shave. This is an individual issue that depends on a girl's personal biology and the degree of her self-consciousness. Think about leaving the door open with words such as, "It looks fine to me, but if you still feel this way come summer, I will consider allowing you to shave then."

"I'm tired all the time."

"I feel tired every day, even when I get enough sleep. I walk around feeling droopy, sleepy, and undependable. I can't sit in the car for 10 minutes without falling asleep. I rarely have an easy time with homework, because I can't concentrate. I love music, but I don't have the energy to practice my instruments anymore. I don't know what I'm dealing with."
Age 10

Dr. Madison: Many girls need more sleep during puberty, some as many as 10 or 11 hours per night, as this is a time of rapid physical growth. This need can pose a challenge to parents. Once children are old enough to do activities and homework at night and get themselves ready for bed, it is easy to get complacent about enforcing a regular bedtime routine. But that might be what this girl needs.

If your daughter is tired all the time, it may be due to the quality of sleep she is getting. Just like an adult, your daughter cannot always catch up on sleep that she loses one night by sleeping longer the next. If she does not sleep solidly for at least four hours, she misses out on REM (or rapid eye movement) sleep, and her sleep is not as restful. Sleep deprivation actually adds up over time. Allowing her to chronically go to bed late during the week or to be wakened by late-night phone calls can have a negative effect on her ability to concentrate and ward off illness, not to mention on her mood!

If her inability to sleep is severe, you may want to talk to her doctor about physical disorders that can affect the quality of sleep. Sleepwalking and sleep *apnea* (a disorder that causes a person to stop breathing temporarily during sleep) can disrupt restful stages of sleep. Illness, stress, or depression also can cause insomnia. In rare instances, a child may suffer from *narcolepsy*, which causes sleep "attacks" during the day during which she cannot stay awake no matter how much sleep she has gotten the night before.

"I'm really tired all the time. I can't go to bed early at night, because there are two televisions in my house so it's too noisy. I try to take naps, but it doesn't work. I sleep late on Saturdays, but that doesn't help. It seems as if I need a different amount of sleep every night. I don't know what to do."
Age 12

Dr. Madison: This girl is giving strong clues about her sleep problem: her household is chaotic. Some people can effectively sleep through noise; others cannot. Children need regular bedtimes that they can stick to, discouragement from napping for longer than 20 to 30 minutes (the nap will affect the quality of sleep at night), and time to unwind before bed. If your daughter has this problem, try turning off the televisions. Read with her or allow her to read on her own, and teach her some stress-reducing techniques such as muscle relaxation or meditation. Also cut down on the caffeinated drinks and chocolate snacks after late afternoon, and emphasize good study habits and not leaving things till the last minute.

"I am proud of my body and what it can do."

"I am really proud of myself and my body. It makes me feel good that my parents tell me I'm beautiful. I felt great at the league track meet— I ran a personal best in the 400-meter dash and it was one of the best days of my life."
Age 14

Dr. Madison: Children want desperately to feel valued. This girl's parents have succeeded in supporting her interest in an activity that emphasizes skill and rewards personal effort. This girl is comfortable with her body and proud of her accomplishments. Participation in sports can encourage your daughter to explore what her body can do and reassure her that a strong and healthy body is not necessarily the skinniest or tiniest one on the team.

"My friends don't understand my health problems."

"I have asthma. My friends say I'm really annoying because I cough and wheeze all the time. The problem is, I can't help it. It's a lot worse for me than it is for them. I don't know whether to feel bad because I'm annoying them or angry at them because they're

*blaming me for something that's
not my fault."*
Age 10

Dr. Madison: Any chronic illness
can limit a young person's activities. It also singles her out as
being different just when she is
trying her best to fit in. Using an
inhaler for asthma is fairly common,
but any illness that requires a
child to do things outside of the
group routine can make her feel
awkward and uncomfortable about
the attention it draws to her,
whether real or imagined. In addition to the hassle of stopping
whatever she is doing to take care
of her illness, your daughter might
worry that others will think she is
faking her symptoms or using
them to avoid activities they think
she does not want to participate
in, such as a gym class or sport.

Give her credit for participating in spite of this difference.
Introduce her to others who have
the same condition. Suggest that
if she treats the need for her
inhaler as ordinary, others eventually will follow her lead. Give her
words to say in response to questions or comments, such as, "When
my asthma flares up, I can't get
enough air. I'll be back out as soon
as the medicine works."

*"I've been deaf in one ear ever since
I was a baby. My friends act like
I'm not there when they talk. When
I ask them to repeat what they say,
they roll their eyes and say, 'Never
mind' and walk away. They treat
me like I'm a baby. I can't help the
way I am."*
Age 12

Dr. Madison: This girl is struggling
with a disability that may or may
not annoy her friends to the degree
she has described. If your daughter
faces a similar struggle, remember
that girls at this age are trying
hard to fit in and are extra sensitive to signals that others are
excluding them. Mention that her
friends probably do not mean to
be as insensitive as they seem
and that they are probably busy
worrying about being accepted
themselves.

If having a hearing device
would not improve the situation,
suggest that your daughter talk
to her friends about helping her
out a little. If some people are
rude to her and will not listen to
her requests to respect her disability, help her focus on those
who are more considerate. Ask
her who seems to be most understanding of her difficulties, and
suggest that she arrange her

physical environment so that someone repeats things for her, stands on her "good ear" side, or catches her up later on what she missed. Remind her that her friends like her in spite of her hearing problem.

"When I first heard the word 'diabetes,' I thought I would cry. I hate having the disease, and I hate being treated differently from everyone else. People make fun of me because of it, and I'm always crying. My parents don't help because there is too much family business going on. I'm really scared and sad. I feel like I'll never be the same again."
Age 10

Dr. Madison: It is normal for a girl with a medical problem that is both dangerous and interferes with normal activities to feel angry and sad. If your daughter deals with a situation like this, she may have loads of questions, but at the same time she may feel that no one can understand what it is like to be in her shoes. As a parent, be extra sensitive to her emotional needs, even if "family business" means your life is already hectic. Help her know that her feelings have merit and that no question is too trivial. Encourage her to write down her thoughts, and then help her to talk to members of her health-care team.

Whether your daughter needs regular insulin injections or extended stays in the hospital, the best approach is to help her educate others. Give her words to respond with, and offer support through listening and understanding. Many communities provide support groups for children with illnesses, where they can find others who share their experiences and concerns. Check with your daughter's physician, with your children's hospital, or in the phone book. If she displays strong feelings of anger, loss, grief, or denial, remember that counseling might give her a chance to explore those emotions in a safe environment. Look for a psychologist or other mental-health professional who has special training and experience with your child's medical condition.

YOUR ROLE

Help her know how to feel good. Teach her the value of exercising regularly, getting enough sleep, and expressing her feelings. Model this for her in your own healthy behavior.

So cry! Let her know there is nothing wrong with a little crying; in fact, a "good cry" can sometimes help her feel better. But also teach her that tears do not substitute for words if she wants you to really understand what is troubling her.

Don't emphasize physical appearance. Home is where a girl should be accepted for who she is and not just for what she looks like. Do not make hurtful comments or demean others for their appearance. Talk about people in terms of their skills, thoughts, and attitudes.

Keep books, magazines, movies, and music appropriate to her age. Girls do not need constant exposure to material that emphasizes physical attractiveness and sexuality. And don't just take some rating service's word for what's appropriate. Know what she is listening to and looking at, and give her input about the messages these media send.

Encourage appropriate dress. As her body changes, help her understand that dressing provocatively sends a message that she wants others to judge her on her sexiness rather than on her personality and accomplishments.

Keep communicating. Puberty involves not only physical development but also changes in emotions, friendships, and other relationships. Your child must be able to trust you and talk to you. Bring up tough subjects. Let her know you care and want to listen.

The Girl in the Mirror

by Carol Eagle, Ph.D.

"I really do not like my appearance. When I get ready for school in the morning, I feel bad when I look in the mirror. Everybody says I'm pretty, but I don't feel like I am. Sometimes how I feel depends on my day. If I've heard negative things from my friends, I may see a negative image that depicts all my flaws. But if I've heard a compliment or two, gotten a new outfit or hairdo, or maybe had an old lady think I was cute and pinch my cheeks, I see a positive, beautiful, flawless image of me. And then some days I look in the mirror and see a mix between the positive and negative. This is the image I am most pleased with, because I believe it's the real me."

age 14

When Alice looked in the mirror in Wonderland, she never knew what she would see. "I wonder if I've been changed in the night!" she says in *Alice's Adventures in Wonderland*.[1] "Let me think: was I the same when I got up this morning? . . . But if I'm not the same, the next question is 'Who in the world am I?' Ah, that's the great puzzle!"

Most girls from age 10 on share Alice's dilemma. Historically, girls have had a difficult time passing through puberty with their

1. Lewis Carroll, *Alice's Adventures in Wonderland* (New York, Smithmark Publishers, 1995): 23.

self-confidence intact. A girl may be confident in her self-image one afternoon, but the next day, after a critical word from a friend or family member, she may doubt not only her attractiveness but also her self-worth.

Today, the greatest challenge girls face is the media's idea of the "beautiful female," an overly thin and glamorized ideal that most girls cannot hope to attain. How can a girl hold on to her sense of self when she faces not only a barrage of unrealistic role models in the media, but also the unsettling hormones coursing covertly through her developing body?

One way to help, of course, is to teach your daughter to say, "I'm not going to fall for all this media hype." As the song goes, "I've gotta be me"—not some facade of a female. Like the girl whose letter opens this chapter, however, your daughter must also learn to deal with criticism from friends, some of whom have already bought into the false ideal. When girls have internalized an unrealistic beauty image, they will hold that mirror up to other girls and pressure them to match the reflection. And almost nothing is more painful for your daughter than a critical word from a friend who thinks your daughter's reflection doesn't measure up.

That's why it's important to teach young girls to look within themselves rather than to others for endorsement. Think of your daughter's self-esteem as a deep well within her, which she can fill with traits of hers that she likes. If it is full, she can draw from it at any time; she doesn't have to wait for an outsider to toss in a compliment. Fill her well by helping her identify what she likes best about her character and her appearance—perhaps her sense of humor and her ambition, as well as her strong arms, bright hazel eyes, and sense of style.

Remembering Her Toddler Years

We parents know we have a difficult job. When our daughters were infants, we literally held their lives in our hands. That responsibility continues as our girls develop. As her parent, you must help your daughter decide what is right for her and what is wrong. You must cope with each and every one of her crises as they appear.

If you were lucky enough to have had an "easy" infant, the first test of your patience and compassion was your daughter's toddlerhood: that time when a perfectly sweet child might suddenly have turned into a tyrannical despot. Reasoning with your toddler got you nowhere. At that stage, your daughter was attempting to move from passive dependence on you to independence. She exerted her new ability to go for whatever she wanted, whether it was the family kitty or an enticing flame flickering on a candle. A toddler's grandiose confidence knows no bounds— but when she falls, she wants only to be the infant secure in her mother's or father's arms.

Girls in adolescence are in a similar bind. They are attempting to strike out on their own. They want to separate from their child-like dependence on their parents and make their own decisions. But these moves are complicated by the radical physical changes they are experiencing. Just as a toddler is unsure of her gait and balance, your young daughter is unsure of her body—the internal messages it sends, as well as how she appears physically to the world.

The combination of your daughter's need for independence and the unsettling physical changes she's experiencing can lead her to outbursts of temper complete with door slamming, nonstop crying over minor slights, or sullen withdrawal. The typical girl brought into my consulting room by her baffled mother is the 13-year-old who used to be such a delight and so easy to get along with. "We were best friends," the mother often says, "but now I can't do anything right. She snaps at everything I do or say."

Although this stage may be painful for you as a parent, it is a necessary developmental step in your daughter's search for her own identity. As a curious toddler, she was fearless until she felt the heat of the candle's flame for herself—and then went running to her parent's arms for comfort. In puberty, your daughter is caught again between two conflicting

"I feel like I have been robbed of my childhood. Most of my life I've looked more mature than my friends. Once someone even asked if I was my sister's mom. I know some girls want to look older than they are, but I just want to look like a kid."
Age 14

forces. She wants to go forward and be her own self, but her body is sending her scary signals that make her want to retreat to the safety of yesteryear.

Time for Straight Talk

You can establish a working relationship with your daughter by talking openly with her about her experiences. The phrase "growing pains" may seem like a handy way to describe what your daughter is experiencing emotionally. In truth, it also reflects her physical experiences: she is gaining height, weight, breasts, hips, and more. Many 13- and 14-year-olds are horrified to see stretch marks appearing on their hips or thighs and feel scarred for life. If your daughter opens the door a bit by asking, "What are these marks?" be ready to address the issue seriously in a conversation about her changing body. Don't ignore her question or joke it away.

As a parent, you must perform a delicate balancing act during this period. You must not be too intrusive, nor can you keep your distance. You have to be ready for a discussion when your daughter is able to ask a question. Think of it as a ballet—a *pas de deux* in which the older, wiser dancer holds the young, coltish neophyte until she gains the ability to dance solo.

You can do this through honest, gentle communication and straight talk. "Straight talk" means staying open to the subjects your daughter wants to discuss, no matter what they are. However, practicing straight talk doesn't require you to be an expert about the workings of the body or talk about something that makes you too uncomfortable.

For example, you might say, "I really don't know the necessary caloric intake for a five-feet-ten-inch 15-year-old girl, so I think we should discuss it with your pediatrician." You should then accompany your daughter to the doctor's office to help her ask this question, because she might never do it on her own, particularly if she is convinced she is overweight.

If your daughter brings up an issue you feel uncomfortable discussing, say so. But then help her find a proper resource for the answer. Would her pediatrician, a good book, or Aunt Sarah have more information? The important message you are communicating is that it is all right to ask questions and be curious. It is good to want to know what's going on with your own body, and there are ways of getting answers—even if Mom or Dad cannot provide them.

Accepting Her Body, Accepting Herself

During this period of growth, your daughter's growing pains don't just hurt or make her feel uncomfortable. They shake the very foundations of the self she has developed. By communicating your awareness of what she may be experiencing physically, you provide her with a safe haven for those times when she feels the need to talk.

Chances are, your daughter doesn't talk to her friends about the eerie sensations and odd physical developments she notices because she fears she is the only one who is experiencing them. You can support her by freely discussing these issues

> *"I'm in fourth grade and my body is already changing. I'm nervous to talk about it, especially with my friends. I'm afraid they will make fun of me. It's embarrassing even with my mom. Is this normal?"*
> Age 10

with her. By bringing them out into the open, you show that she should not be afraid or ashamed of them.

If you feel handcuffed by your daughter's reluctance to talk, the best way to approach appearance-related subjects is to talk about other girls—girls on TV, real girls, girls you knew and the women they became, yourself included. The last idea is tricky; if you put yourself into the equation too much, your daughter may dismiss your experience, considering it irrelevant to today's times.

It does work, though, if you are able to talk about your embarrassment over having been "too" something—too fat, too tall, and so forth. Choose some physical characteristic that your daughter does not worry about, and talk about how you dealt with your own feelings on that subject. Describe how you felt when you worried you wouldn't grow anymore: "I've always wanted to be tall, like you are. It made me feel so inferior to my friends when I was 14 years old and much shorter than they were." Or, "When my breasts first grew, I got round-shouldered hiding them. I'm so glad you don't feel that way. You have such good posture."

Openly admire aspects of your daughter's appearance that are quite different from your own. If you are shorter than she is, admire her height, even if she feels too tall and gangly. This helps her experience her individuality and her separateness from you.

Whether your daughter is concerned with her weight, height, or flat chest, you can approach her concern by sharing the facts of genetically determined body structure. Talk with her positively about whether she favors your side of the family or her father's. Use a relative that you know your daughter admires as a reference point. If your daughter feels her nose is too big, put your arm around her and look into the mirror together. Tell her, "I see the same strength in your face that I see in Aunt Marie's." If you're her father, let her know how proud you are to see some of your own characteristics in her face.

Her Personal Taste

Then there is the delicate issue of what to do when you feel your daughter *doesn't* look all right—maybe because of acne or because of the clashing colors of her outfit. The acne should be treated as you would a medical problem that is not appearance related. A specialist should be consulted about her specific condition, just as you would consult an orthopedist if she had a broken ankle.

But what if the problem is a matter of taste or style? If the colors of her outfit clash, grin and bear it, but note to yourself that she may need more exposure to the aesthetics of clothing. Acknowledge that styles change and that what you think looks good is not necessarily what she thinks is in style. If her clothing is too risqué or sexy, have a discussion on what message the outfit

> *"I can't wear funky shoes or get my ears pierced because my mom thinks I'm too young. I feel very left out, and my mom doesn't understand. I don't think I can wait until I'm 13 like she wants."*
> Age 11

sends to others. Ask her what she thinks; she may not realize the power of her body or how others may interpret her style. Your 12-year-old may want to look 16 because it's the "in" style, and she may succeed. But emotionally, she's still 12. Explain that girls who dress sexy may face pressures they are not ready to handle.

A big issue today is body piercing and tattooing. Most girls first raise the issue of body piercing by expressing their desperate need to get their ears pierced. That is the prime time to open an ongoing discussion about altering one's body—your feelings about it, your family's attitudes, health and medical concerns, and your cultural values. When she comes back later wanting multiple ear piercings, a navel ring, or a tattoo, some groundwork will have been laid. This is particularly important today because of society's emphasis on making the body beautiful through surgery. By starting the conversation over pierced ears, you can set the stage for later discussions about breast enhancement, nose jobs, and more.

No matter how much your daughter denigrates your positive input, keep it up, and keep the channels of communication open. Your daughter's transformation into a young woman—even with its moments of awkwardness and difficulty—will be an incredible thing to watch. If you can help her not only accept but also relish herself now (and you can!), as she grows, you'll be able to stand back and watch her take flight.

Dr. Carol Eagle is the retired head of the Department of Child and Adolescent Psychology at Montefiore Medical Center in New York and the author of the book **All That She Can Be: Helping Your Daughter Maintain Her Self-Esteem.** *She runs a group therapy program for 11- to 13-year-old girls out of her private practice.*

LISTENING IN

Dr. Eagle shares advice on girls' concerns about body image, peer pressure to dress "right," dealing with compliments, and how girls feel when they look in the mirror.

"What is 'pretty,' anyway?"

"The model image is so overrated. Just because all girls don't wear a size two and aren't six feet tall doesn't mean we're not beautiful. A lot of models have eating disorders and are unhappy with themselves. Girls shouldn't try to change their bodies or have plastic surgery to look like models. Being on the cover of a magazine doesn't mean a thing."
Age 13

Dr. Eagle: This girl believes the media's definition of beauty is too narrow, and that's a positive sign. She can redefine attractiveness to include people who look more like herself and her friends. It may also be reassuring for her to think models have eating disorders; it lets her hold on to her self-confidence, particularly if, like most girls, her figure doesn't match up to the ones portrayed in the media.

If your daughter feels distressed that she doesn't have the figure of a model or the shining teeth or gorgeous hair of her favorite actress, explore examples of real-life beauty with her. You might ask, "Have you noticed how pretty my friend Lynne is? But you'd never see someone her size or shape in a magazine. I don't think that's right. What do you think?" This can get you to the core issue: that how you feel, carry, and present yourself is the real issue in attractiveness.

"I am Korean. The girls I see on television and in movies are usually blonde and slim. I don't see many girls who look like me."
Age 10

Dr. Eagle: In spite of progress made to have more ethnically diverse casts in film and television, there is still far to go. If your daughter feels similarly left out, support her perception that even as the media features more ethnically diverse women, they still predominantly use tall and skinny as the criteria for beauty. Find out who *she* thinks is attractive that does not meet the tall-and-skinny criteria. Ask what she would do if *she* was the director of a film or television

series. This can help you get into her feelings of strangeness or inequities in life.

"I hate my weight."
"I weigh 120 pounds. My parents and my brother say that I should lose weight, but my friends say I shouldn't. I'm hurt that my parents and brother say this because the translation is 'You're fat!' "
Age 12

Dr. Eagle: Listen to the pain in this girl's voice. When her parents criticize her, she feels as if she has no support at home: she cannot confide in her parents about her fears and supposed shortcomings. When her weight becomes a topic of family discussion, she feels as if her family is ganging up on her.

Generally, 12-year-olds have "bumpy" figures because they're in puberty. If your daughter is not concerned about her size, wait until she's a little older, age 14 or 15, to talk about what you perceive as a weight problem.

If she thinks she is overweight, though, she is hurting and needs to talk. Remember that when you discuss food issues, you're talking about more than nutrition—you're talking about her feelings, which may include guilt, frustration,

embarrassment, and insecurity. This is not the time to lecture; let her talk, and listen with respect.

"I don't know what's wrong with me—I have a huge gut. I weigh 105 pounds, but I should only weigh about 94 pounds. People say I'm skinny, but they only say it to make me feel better. I'm embarrassed to wear a bathing suit. I've tried lots of exercises and I eat right. My mom doesn't want me to take drugs to lose weight, but I don't know what else I should try. I've done everything else."
Age 11

Dr. Eagle: Since this girl's weight is not high and other people tell her she's skinny, she is almost certainly exaggerating her size. But telling your daughter she's not fat when she thinks she is will only get you stuck in a circuitous "Yes, I am," "No, you're not" argument. Such complaints often hide hurt feelings. Explore her emotions with "Are you upset about something?" or "It sounds as if you're hurting." Then empathize with her pain if she has been insulted or injured emotionally.

Diet drugs would be an extraordinary measure for an 11-year-old. Although many girls are drawn to diet pills and supplements, pediatricians rarely prescribe them to young people because the drugs contain powerful amphetamines, and their long-term effect on development is not yet understood. Some weight-loss aids contain *ephedra*, a powerful stimulant responsible for a number of emergency-room visits and even deaths. The more-is-better philosophy kids employ often leads them to take more of these drugs and supplements than needed, which makes them particularly dangerous.

"I may have an eating disorder."

"I eat constantly, and I think it's time for me to stop eating altogether. Not only do I eat bad things, but I eat too much of them. Last summer I was on the swim team. I lost weight then, but I don't want to go out for it this year. My mom says I should, not just because I'm heavy, but to exercise. I have gained 35 pounds in one year. I'm ashamed of it, but I can't stop eating."
Age 12

Dr. Eagle: In puberty, many girls experience an increased appetite. If they don't understand that this is a biological fact, they may feel as if their bodies are careening out of control. It's important that you matter-of-factly accept your daughter's change in appetite, rather than get alarmed by it.

Many girls give up their athletic ambitions when they are around 12 years old, often because they're afraid of calling attention to their changing bodies. If your daughter wants to drop out of a sport she used to enjoy, do whatever you can to keep her involved, or help her explore another sport. Routinely make at least one athletic endeavor part of the schedule for everybody in the household. If you get out and exercise regularly—even without your daughter—you don't need to lecture. Research shows that mothers who model healthy choices have a positive effect on their daughters' activity levels.

"I have been bulimic since I was 12. I throw up almost everything I eat, and I've just begun taking laxatives when I can't throw up. My friends are beginning to pay more attention to me, and I'm getting nervous. I want to stop, sort of, but I'm afraid that if I do, I'll gain a lot of weight."
Age 13

"I have to be in control of my body and grades. If I get a single B in school, my grade-point average will

be ruined, colleges won't give me a scholarship, and all my dreams will be shattered. I can't let that happen. I know I'm capable of molding and changing my body, and it makes me happier when I have that control. It's dangerous, but I just can't have it any other way."
Age 14

Dr. Eagle: Some girls feel controlling their weight is a way to gain power over other aspects of their lives. If your daughter shows signs of anorexia nervosa or bulimia nervosa, consult a mental health professional immediately. Although you may hope you can handle the problem privately at home, all your love can't cure your daughter.

Eating disorders are too complex to respond to simple family concern. Anorexics deny their hunger through self-starvation because of an irrational fear of getting fat. Bulimics go on eating binges and then purge through vomiting or use of laxatives or diuretics. A parent who rewards

---

Warning Signs for Anorexia and Bulimia

Anorexia Nervosa
If your daughter:

- deliberately starves herself
- has an intense, persistent fear of gaining weight
- refuses to eat except for tiny portions
- diets continuously
- has excessive facial or body hair
- exercises compulsively
- shows abnormal weight loss
- seems especially sensitive to cold
- has irregular or absent menstruation
- shows signs of hair loss

Bulimia Nervosa
If your daughter:

- seems preoccupied with food
- hides food in her room
- hurries to the bathroom after meals
- abuses laxatives, diuretics, or diet pills
- denies her hunger
- exercises compulsively
- has broken blood vessels in her eyes
- has a rash on her knuckles, frequent sore throats, or swollen glands

*National Association of Anorexia Nervosa and Associated Disorders

or punishes a child for weight gain can unknowingly launch her into a cycle of eating disorders. Most large hospitals have eating disorder centers that offer a variety of individual and group treatments.

"I'm too tall (or too short)!"

"I've always been taller than my best friend, but this summer I shot up like a bean stalk. I'm taller than most people in my class now, and I don't like it. I feel embarrassed to be around my best friend, who is much shorter than I am. She doesn't seem to mind, but I do."
Age unknown

Dr. Eagle: Being able to look down at the top of her friend's head isn't the only thing this girl is worried about. A girl who sprouts several inches in a short period of time may feel awkward in many ways, not just with her height. Her coordination may have been thrown off, and she is in the process of adapting all her musculature—and her brain—to this new body.

If your daughter is in this situation, remind her that eventually some classmates will catch up to her in height. Ease her embarrassment by pointing out successful tall women in your family, among friends, or in the media. Help her

coordination by working with her on a sport or other physical activity you can do together at home—especially one in which height is an advantage.

"I'm four feet four inches tall, and everyone treats me like a little kid just because I'm short. I don't whine, and I try to show people that I'm smarter than I look. People judge me by my size instead of by my brain."
Age 12

Dr. Eagle: While their tall friends deal with feeling too conspicuous, short girls worry about not being taken seriously. Girls ages 10 to 13 are especially concerned about being short because, at a time when they want only to be a teenager, they fear they'll be tagged "kids." And being a kid doesn't give a girl the respect and independence she craves.

If you are concerned that your daughter is smaller than her peers, consult a pediatrician to learn more about her expected growth. She may still have a growth spurt ahead of her. Encourage her to map out a strategy for responding to teasing. Start with naming famous short people—like figure skater Tara Lipinski (five feet one) or writer Laura Ingalls Wilder (about four feet eleven). Discuss with your daughter how she is part of a whole world of short people who have accomplished great things.

"What's with all these changes in my body?"

"I'm going into fourth grade, and I'm developing. I don't know what to do. Here are some reasons why I don't like it:
1. I like to sleep on my stomach at night, and it bothers me now.
2. My family always interrupts me right when I'm about to take a bath and I don't have a shirt on.
3. I JUST DON'T LIKE IT!"
Age unknown

Dr. Eagle: Girls who express these kinds of thoughts are feeling emotional discomfort as much as physical. If your daughter is an early bloomer, talk with her about her development. Do her breasts hurt, or does she really need to talk about how strange her body is feeling these days? Does she think she will have her period soon? Is she afraid of developing before her friends do? If other family members developed early, reassure her by sharing their experiences.

Girls at this age have every right to expect some privacy. Everyone in a family needs a private place, and the bathroom is usually off-limits to other family members. Help your family respect your daughter's need at this delicate time in her development.

"Should I feel good about getting compliments?"

"There are times I feel good about myself and other times I feel depressed—it all depends on my surroundings and the people I am with. I feel good when my parents tell me I am beautiful, or when my friends say they are envious of how skinny I am. Even when they say that, though, sometimes I just don't feel like believing them."
Age 14

Dr. Eagle: This girl is basing a good part of her self-confidence on others' praise, and that's a slippery slope to be on. When the compliments aren't frequent enough or the kind she wants to hear, her self-confidence may take a nosedive.

Help your daughter feel confident for reasons other than her looks. She should be proud of her achievements—acing an exam or trying hard in a game—not just her appearance. Regularly praise her intelligence, sense of humor, and abilities without bringing up looks.

"Everyone else wears makeup."

"Lots of girls in my class wear makeup. I don't, because my parents don't like it. They say, 'Girls who wear makeup to school are just trying to get the boys' attention. You're only 10 years old!' There's a ton of pressure between girls who wear makeup and the teachers. They think girls who wear makeup are trying to say, 'We're all that.'"

Age 10

Dr. Eagle: If your daughter feels ostracized because you won't allow makeup at a young age, think through your position. If you feel strongly that she should wait, stand your ground, but have good reasons. Put your position in the context of other females in your family: "Your aunt, grandma, and I think makeup should be a rite of passage. You can start wearing it on your thirteenth birthday." Your daughter may not understand the power of the message makeup can send. She may feel it helps her create a new self at a time when she feels insecure. Tell her, "When you wear heavy makeup, people may think you are older and ready for things you don't want to do."

It may be better to yield somewhat on this issue than to have your daughter sneak around your rules. Consider allowing only nail polish or light lip gloss when she's younger, and remember: many girls this age give up makeup after trying it briefly. They find it's just too much work to mess around with on a daily basis.

"Is being cool all that matters?"

"Once a girl came up to me and asked me if I shopped at Zutopia or Abercrombie. I said no. She asked, 'Then where do you shop?' I said, 'At the Gap.' She asked me, 'Do you consider yourself cool?' When I said no, she said, 'Good. 'Cause you're not.' I felt like marching up to her and telling her that she should just learn to be nice. Period."

Age 9

Dr. Eagle: If your daughter experiences situations like this, encourage her to take pride in the choices she makes. Support her efforts to stand up for herself, and discuss how they are more valuable than doing what the "cool girl" does. Try to assess how your daughter feels about the girl who made the remark. It can be hard for your daughter to take pride in independent choices if she secretly admires this other girl.

"I wish I didn't have this tattoo."
"I have a tattoo of a butterfly on my back. I wish I didn't have it because now I'm stuck with it forever. The procedure was painful and expensive. I don't think it was worth the time, pain, or money."
Age 13

Dr. Eagle: Like this girl, your daughter may be dealing with the desire to participate in trends like tattooing and body piercing—or coping with the repercussions of already having done so. If she is under tremendous pressure to join her friends in this kind of body art, coming down adamantly against it will invite her teenage rebellious self to go ahead and do it anyway—or to adorn an area she can hide from your eyes. To her, these trends can signal control over her body and membership in a community of peers. You are right to want her to be safe and wise in her choices. But do try to embrace the person she wants to be. If you think she's too young for the act now, let her know you'll reconsider when she's older.

If your daughter wants body art you object to, talk with her about medical concerns. The tattooing and piercing industries are largely unregulated, and unclean settings and unsterilized equipment can lead to infection. More than 20 states have laws about piercing minors, but they may not be enforced. As the girl in this letter points out, these are not fashion statements your daughter can easily erase. Talk about the permanency of the acts: tattoo removal can include risk of scarring, and piercings in damp areas like the tongue and cheek do not heal as easily as a hole in the ear. Visit her doctor and dentist together to learn more about medical issues, including tattoo removal.

YOUR ROLE

Try to see her as she sees herself. Have your daughter tell you what she sees in her reflection, and describe the positive things you see in her face.

Praise character more than looks. Make 80 percent of what you say focus on who she is and less than 20 percent on what she looks like.

Talk about friends. Examine her friend's choices, but don't compare your daughter to her. "I noticed Abby looks thinner. Is she trying to lose weight? Does she talk about it?" This can ease the way into talking about herself.

Watch how you talk about yourself. Be honest about your own figure flaws, but also talk about your personality and character strengths.

Look in the news. Find out what she thinks about a new acne treatment or breast reduction method. Conversations that aren't personal allow you both to express opinions on a neutral playing field.

Speak up, dads! A father's praise of a girl's appearance and character can boost her self-confidence in an enduring way. Dad shouldn't comment on particular body parts or her shape; he should simply let her know how beautiful she is in his eyes.

If your daughter wants plastic surgery, listen closely. What problem does she think it will solve? Does she think having a nose like her favorite actress will improve her social life? Uncover the underlying issues—and counter them. Also remind your daughter that it's normal not to like all her features now and that she should give herself time to grow into her body.

Appreciate diversity. Discuss what you find beautiful about people with varying body types, styles, and skin tones. Help her see that women of all shapes and sizes can be beautiful.

Family Life
by Evelyn Bassoff, Ph.D.

"My older brothers drive me crazy. My parents are divorced,
and we live with my mom. When I try to be nice to my brothers,
they're mean. Sometimes they won't talk to me, and that gives
me a huge headache. We always fight! I try to count to ten to cool
off, but I'm so tired of it. At times I get so mad, I say mean things
back to them. I try to control my anger, but it gets to the point
where nothing seems to help."

Age unknown

During our daughters' preteen and teen years, two compelling and often conflicting wishes shape their behavior. On the one hand, they yearn for close, warm relationships in the family. On the other hand, they are intent on asserting their differences and independence. It's not an easy trick to be close and distant at the same time—Houdini himself would have been daunted. That is one reason adolescence is such a trial for them and for us.

The girl whose letter opens this chapter yearns for closeness with her brothers and a more peaceful family life. Yet she can't help but push back against her brothers' manipulation as she struggles for her own rights. Her inability to have control over the situation fills her with an anger that is just plain wearing her out.

From the time girls are infants and forever after, relating will be central to their very being. More so than males, females define themselves in the context of relationship—whether as daughter, sister, friend, girlfriend, wife, or mother. They also judge themselves in terms of their ability to care about others. Talking through problems, making peace, and understanding the people closest to them are skills that enhance their self-worth. On the contrary, not having connection brings on feelings of personal failure.

I'm concerned that unless our letter writer learns how to stand up to her brothers effectively, she'll continue to internalize her anger (as many girls do) and make herself sick. Like so many girls in this age group, she would benefit from learning assertiveness skills, and if her parents are at a loss here, a professional counselor could help.

"I am me, not you!"

As much as our teenage daughters value emotional intimacy and loving relationships within the family, they also want to feel separate and different from us. "I am me, not you," my own daughter, then age 15, blurted out, tears streaming down her face, after a relative had remarked on our physical resemblance.

The major developmental task your daughter must master during adolescence is forming her own unique, firm sense of self—an identity separate from you and her siblings. During this process, which already began in the preteen years, she is discovering her own beliefs, values, wishes, desires, talents, and dreams. She is learning to find her own way in the world and develop confidence that she can survive outside the protective family circle. "Leave me alone," "Don't try to run my life," or "Stop snooping," she may loudly insist as she wrenches herself away from your protection and control.

How can you help your daughter through her separation struggles and survive this tumultuous time yourself? Reassure her that the inner turmoil she is experiencing is normal and healthy. "I know this is not an easy time for you," you can tell her. "One minute, you want to be a little girl and for us to be very close. The next minute, everything we do gets on your nerves and you want us out of your life. But then you feel guilty because you really don't want to hurt our feelings. Honey, you've got one foot in the land of childhood and the other foot in the land of adulthood. That's why being a teenager is so tough."

> *"I am the oldest in my family. Recently, my little sister was learning how to read, and I felt bad because my mom was spending a lot of time with her. She used to do that with me when I was little, and I felt left out. To make myself feel better, I started keeping a journal. When I write about my emotions, it makes me feel important."*
> Age 12

You can also take your daughter's rejections of you less personally. It's the parent part, not the human part, that she's pushing away. Her insults, eye rolling, and disapproval will also sting less when you remember that she has to find fault with you because if you remained perfect in her eyes, she'd never muster the courage to leave you.

Mothers and Fathers

More than anyone else in the world, a mother threatens her daughter's struggle to become an adult. It's not because we mothers connive to hold our daughters back. It's because we are continual reminders that not so very long ago, they were part of us— safe, warm, and shielded from the outside world. We carried them in our bodies, nursed and nourished them, and were attuned to their every movement and mood. For young girls, growing up means they have to give up their childish dependence on us, though part of them secretly still wants it. To this end, they create distance between themselves and us.

Although teenage daughters also wrestle to break away from their fathers, friction between fathers and daughters is sometimes less irritating than that between mothers and daughters. Dad and daughter may often butt heads, but a young girl feels inherently different from her male parent. She does not have to struggle to disidentify with him as she does with her mother. Around Dad she can relax, and she will find it easier to accept his guidance, support, and advice. During this stormy period of her life, Dad can be a safe harbor—a place to go when the relationship with Mom is too intense.

The Brother-Sister Bond

The girl whose letter opens this chapter struggles with her brothers, but growing up with boys needn't be a miserable experience for your daughter. In fact, as long as mutual respect and love predominate in your family, having a brother is a plus for your daughter. Being around a boy so much of the time, she learns to feel comfortable in the company of the opposite sex, which will make it easier for her to communicate with boyfriends as a teenager.

Because she is privy to her brother's vulnerabilities, she also learns that although guys may be tough on the outside, they're usually pretty tender on the inside. This bit of wisdom will encourage her to have compassion for males. Additionally, by having to deal with her brother's teasing and joking, she learns to be resilient, to develop a sense of humor, and not to take personally every little slight.

But let's not forget that while it's normal for a boy to tease his sister, it's not normal to torment her. Parents need to distinguish between healthy "boy energy" that may be raucous but is not violent or sadistic, and "crazy" boy energy that is destructive, degrading, and dominating. Just as you need to stop your son from harming your daughter—or get professional help if you can't be effective—you also need to intervene when your daughter maliciously taunts her brother. Sibling squabbling is a fact of family life, but sibling cruelty is never acceptable.

Sister to Sister

Relationships between sisters are no less complicated than those between sisters and brothers. In fact, sisters will bicker even more: "No! You can't borrow my green sweater." "They're *my* friends, not yours." "Get out of my room, and stay out!" What often provokes the tension between young girls is their need to see themselves as separate and different from one another. Every teenage girl wants to believe she is unique and special, and for this reason, your daughter may balk at sharing her personal possessions, her friends, or her personal space with her sister.

Though you may be keenly aware that your daughter is struggling to differentiate herself from you, you may not realize she may also be struggling to separate from her sister. Once she is sure that she is not her sister's clone, she can stop struggling and allow the closeness and warmth they both long for. Not surprisingly, sisters often develop deep and lifelong friendships.

"Only" Children

A daughter who doesn't have brothers or sisters is spared the bickering that normally goes on between siblings. Not having a rival for Mom's or Dad's love, she basks in the glory of being Number One. An "only daughter" often struggles with feeling too important to her parents rather than not important enough. Unlike a daughter from a bigger family, she may feel solely responsible for her parents' happiness. She may worry that if she doesn't measure up in this way or that, she will cause her parents sorrow and disappointment. Or she may worry that if she doesn't hang out with Mom and Dad, she'll be lonely. For this reason and many others, it is vital that parents lead a full life, one rich in friendships and meaningful activities. In this way, they show their daughter they don't depend on her for their emotional well-being.

Sometimes the parents of "onlies" are concerned that their child won't develop the social skills that a child with siblings has. Not to worry. As long as she has opportunities to be with other kids in school and other activities, she'll do fine making friends and figuring out what works and what doesn't work socially.

Marriage and Divorce

During the emotional roller-coaster ride that is adolescence, family stability takes on new importance. An intact family gives a teenager confidence that she will be able to venture out into the world, knowing fully that when she needs comfort, home will still be there for her to return to.

Adolescence is also that stage when a girl daydreams about falling in love. If her parents are married, a girl learns by example that promises are kept, commitments are real, and marital conflicts are resolvable. How you interact as a married couple also influences your daughter's expectations for herself. If you and your spouse treat each other with respect, your daughter is more likely

> *"My parents seem to have a very good relationship. They get into occasional fights, but they seem like best friends most of the time. That's why I love them so much."*
> *age 13*

to model and expect this behavior in her relationships.

Unfortunately, not all married couples make it, and divorce is a fact of life. Conventional wisdom used to hold that it was better for the kids when incompatible spouses split up. Now we know it's not that simple. Though adults may measure their happiness by how fulfilled they are in their marriages, children are far less concerned with this. As long as there is no violence between their parents, what kids desperately want is for their parents to stay together through thick and thin. That way their lives won't be disrupted and they will be adequately cared for. But some marriages are simply not workable, and ending the relationship becomes the only reasonable solution.

In a divorcing family, one of the major problems for a young girl is that Mom and Dad, overwhelmed by the stresses they face, do not have the energy to provide her with the parental guidance, support, and supervision she needs. For this reason, it can help to bring other sensitive and responsible grown-ups into their daughter's life. Grandparents, loving relatives and friends, and counselors can become comforting and valuable resources.

Another risk factor is that a young girl will be caught in the cross fire of hostilities and pressured to reject one of her parents. Although one parent may secretly hope the other parent falls off the face of the earth, their daughter's self-image will always be tied to her relationship with both parents. She wants to be loved by them both and to love them both.

If you divorce, your daughter deserves a full explanation for the

"I hate the way that my separated parents communicate with each other. I wish I could live with someone else besides either of them, but it's out of the question. Meanwhile, I'm stuck with holding my ears until they can put their differences aside and act like adults."
Age 14

painful disruption of her life. When a child of any age believes her parents are making the decision to divorce impulsively, she cannot help but feel that her world is dangerously out of control. Especially during the maelstrom of the preteen and teen years, your daughter needs to trust that her parents are rational, that life makes sense, and that there is order in the world. Ideally, you can truthfully tell her that you and your former spouse tried your best to stay together and undertook the drastic step of divorce only after all other efforts had failed.

The divorce experience is not a single event for your daughter. It is a process that begins with the growing rift between you and your spouse and resolves with her acceptance of her postdivorce family, which may include stepparents, stepsiblings, and half siblings. We must remember that although a remarriage can enhance the well-being of the parent, it is not always the best situation for our children. For some children of divorce, becoming integrated into a new family is simply overwhelming. It's a major change in their lives that they are unable to cope with. For other children, a parent's remarriage can bring a welcome sense of security and stability. In my experience as a therapist, I have come to believe that mothers and fathers who work hard to know their children are able to tell what they can handle and what is too much for them.

The failure of your marriage does not doom your daughter to a similar fate. Although many children of divorce do become cynical about love and marriage and are sometimes afraid to enter a life-long commitment themselves, many others do not lose their capacity for enduring, intimate relationships. In fact, living through a divorce and the terrible human pain that accompanies it may result in greater compassion and psychological understanding in some children of divorce.

Respecting Her Identity and Space

It is both scary and exciting to grow up. Teenage girls are plagued with doubts about their self-worth: *I'll never be as smart as my sister. Do I have any real talents? Are my parents disappointed in me? Will I be able to take care of myself when I leave home?*

You can't take away all your daughter's insecurities, though your heart may break when she's down on herself. However, you can enhance her self-confidence by loving her for who she is, by recognizing her accomplishments and accepting her failures. You can also avoid doing what crushes her spirit: comparing her to her sibling, expecting her to carry on in a sibling's footsteps, and insisting she lead the life you think would be best for her.

Adolescence is a time of transformation. Your daughter needs her private space and hours alone to daydream, write in her diary, and problem solve. And she needs to keep secrets from you. After all, even if you are her parent, you don't have the right to peer into her soul. When I told my daughter, a woman of 29 and soon to be a mother herself, about the chapter on family I was writing for this book, I asked her what she needed most from me when she was a teenager. She answered without hesitation: "My privacy."

> *"My mom is always reading my diary and snooping around my room. Nobody even knocks on my door before they come in. It's really getting on my nerves. I feel like I'm going to explode! I've wanted so many times to give my mother a piece of my mind. I don't even care how much trouble I would get into."*
> Age 14

Dr. Evelyn Bassoff is a practicing psychologist, a mother, and the author of several parenting books, including **Mothers and Daughters: Loving and Letting Go** *and* **Cherishing Our Daughters: How Parents Can Raise Girls to Become Confident Women.** *For seven years, she was the "Marriage and Sex" columnist for* Parents *magazine.*

LISTENING IN

Lack of privacy, battles with siblings, concerns about their parents' marriage . . . Dr. Bassoff reflects on the struggles adolescent girls experience within their family life.

"No one respects my privacy."
"I live in a house full of seven people, and everyone just walks in my room. I ask them nicely not to and tell them how I feel. I even put my bed and a trash can against the door, but they still push the door open. I need my privacy!"
Age 11

Dr. Bassoff: It's natural to want to love and protect your children, but sometimes we parents fall short on giving them what they also need: boundaries that separate them from us. This girl is pleading with her family to respect her normal and healthy wish for privacy, but no one is taking her seriously. Developmentally, she is right on track. But it may be that the other people in the family still think of her as the little girl who never used to keep them out.

So what's behind this insistence on privacy? Starting in the preteen years, a girl wants the right to close her bedroom door, knowing that no one will intrude on her. Her room is ideally a place that is safe from the curious and peering eyes of her family members: a place where she can fantasize, problem solve, listen to "her" music, sing, dance, gaze at herself in the mirror, examine her changing body, talk to herself, write in her journal, and reach deep down into her soul to discover its innermost truths.

Is retreating from the family a good idea? Yes. In a study of 31 eminent women, including Eleanor Roosevelt, Marie Curie, and Maya Angelou, researcher Barbara Kerr discovered what they all had in common was ample opportunity to be by themselves: a protected, private, quiet space in which to grow. [1]

"I got in a big fight with my parents when they said they had

1. Barbara Kerr, *Smart Girls, Gifted Women* (Dayton: Ohio Psychology Press, 1985).

the right to go through my things any time they wanted. Now I don't ever trust my parents with anything of mine that is private."
Age 14

Dr. Bassoff: Most teenage girls want to be close with their parents but not too close. As your daughter matures, you may find that she is willing to be open with you, as long as she is not coerced. Forcing your way in may only push her away.

When your daughter was a child, you needed to be informed about all aspects of her life. Now that she is an adolescent, be willing to give up the right to know all and honor the boundaries that separate her from you. Of course, you should be sure to keep your "danger" eyes open; safety always takes precedence over privacy. We should not kid ourselves—diminishing our power as parents is not easy for us! But the reward is a daughter who has the space and time to bloom into the unique, independent soul you ultimately want her to be.

"My brothers and sisters are driving me crazy."

"My little sister and I haven't been getting along very well. When she gets frustrated or mad, she scratches and hits me. She doesn't listen, so I pin her down to control her from hitting me. When my mom hears her screaming 'Let go,' she walks in and thinks I am the one hurting my sister. I try telling my mom, but she always says, 'I don't want to hear it,' and then I get in trouble."
Age 11

Dr. Bassoff: This girl is overwhelmed because she doesn't know how to protect herself from her scrappy little sister. It doesn't take long to learn that getting in the middle of siblings' problems can make things worse. But sometimes our children do need us to intervene. All too often, the older sibling gets the blame because a parent overlooks how provocative the younger sibling is. If your older daughter expresses similar frustrations, instead of saying, "I don't want to hear it," give her tools to deal with her kid sister.

You might say, "I know your little sister can be a pest, but you can't get physical with her. You can say, 'Look, I'll hang out with you, but only if you're nice to me.' Or you can simply walk away from her. You can also try looking her in the eye and telling her in

a stern voice, 'We don't scratch or hit in this family.' If none of these strategies work, you can always come to me and ask me to handle her because she's out of control."

"My sister and I are adopted. She is black and I am white. I am really mean to her, and I don't know why! Could I be racist? I really don't think I am, but am I?"
Age 13

Dr. Bassoff: Adolescence is an especially difficult time for an adopted daughter and for her adoptive parents. In discovering who she is—one of the central tasks of adolescence—an adopted daughter will become intensely interested in her origins. "Just who was the woman who gave birth to me? Why did she give me up?" she asks herself. The adopted teenager may come to believe in her heart that she was defective in some basic way. As she processes these feelings and mourns the loss of her first mother, she may experience feelings of shame and low self-esteem.

Teenagers often mask their sad feelings with angry ones, and when they lash out, they hurt the people closest to them—particularly parents and siblings. Our letter writer may resent her sister for being black, but not because she is a racist, as she fears. It may be that she hates the fact that her family is "different." She may secretly wonder why they can't look like a "normal" family.

Talking on a regular basis about all the mixed-up feelings that go along with being adopted and part of an interracial family is the best way to help your adopted daughters feel safe, loved, and accepted. Some adoptive parents find that family counseling is also helpful, because the counselor makes sure that the uncomfortable, painful things that need to be said and heard will be.

"I want my sibling to like me."
"My big sister and I don't get along at all! Well, really, she doesn't get along with me. Every time I wear the same thing she wears, she freaks out. I try to be nice, but every time I talk to her, she gets mean. I wish that for at least one day, we could get along."
Age unknown

Dr. Bassoff: It's painful for parents to see one of their children being rejected by another. The older sister clearly wants to be seen as her own unique person, which is why she has a fit when the younger one dresses like her. The younger sister looks up to the older one, which is why she copies her sister's style.

If your daughters are in a similar situation, set aside an uninterrupted 30 minutes for a family meeting. Tell your daughters: "You two are very different. I respect and love both of you, but the way you're acting is making family life a misery for all of us. We have to have some ground rules that will help you get along better."

Advise your younger daughter just how she must respect her sister's privacy—tell her that her big sister's room is off-limits and that she must ask permission to enter and to borrow clothes. Explain to your older daughter that her younger sister needs to be shown more kindness and consideration. Ask your daughters if they have other ideas to make their relationship work better, and talk about these together. Initiating family projects and activities that call for teamwork between the girls—such as wilderness camping, painting a room, planting a garden, or decorating the house for a birthday or holiday celebration—might also help them to feel more like friends than adversaries.

"What can I do to help?"

"My sister has a neuromuscular disease. She is 11, but she has the mind of a four-year-old. I really love her! Lots of people, including my next-door neighbors, stare and make fun of her. I really hate that. What should I do to prevent it from happening? For the last two years I've been yelling at them, and I don't want to do that anymore."
Age 9

Dr. Bassoff: Having a disabled sister has enlarged this young girl's capacity for tenderness and protectiveness. It has also exposed her to other people's insensitivity and cruelty toward people with disabilities. Be specific and tell your daughter exactly what she might say when she is confronted with hurtful remarks. She might respond politely but firmly, "My sister has feelings just like you. Please don't make fun of her." Or, "I'd appreciate it if you wouldn't stare at my sister because it makes us both uncomfortable."

One way of practicing new scripts is through role-playing.

The child can take the part of the offending person, and the parent can take the part of the child. Then the roles can be reversed. Of course, sometimes the safest response is to ignore an offensive person. We need to impress upon our daughters that if they feel threatened in any way, they should walk away rather than confront.

"I'm scared. I just found out that two of my three sisters have had eating disorders. One had bulimia and the other had anorexia. My third sister has depression. I want my family to be more open with me. I think I should have known about these things when they began. What if something else is going on behind my back?"
Age unknown

Dr. Bassoff: Sometimes in our efforts to protect our child from unhappiness, we hide family members' problems. As a result, our child usually experiences more anxiety rather than less. After all, it is the unknown, not the known, that makes us irrationally afraid. This girl wants to know what's been going on, and in a calm and truthful manner, her parents ought to tell her. They can also tell her how she can be a friend to her troubled sisters, and that it's okay for her to enjoy her life even though a family member is ill.

This girl is also worried—with good reason—that she may follow in her sisters' footsteps. It may be a good idea to enlist the help of a therapist who can explain eating disorders (which are very complicated) and help this girl find ways to stay healthy—and to nip in the bud any emotional or psychological problems that she may face down the line.

"I am *not* like my sister."

"My mom and dad always compare me to my older sister. They expect me to be able to do the same things she could do at my age and to have the same interests. I want to tell my parents that I want to be different."
Age 10

Dr. Bassoff: Every parent knows that comparing one child to another is wrong, wrong, wrong. Yet we can't always help ourselves; sometimes we slip and do this very thing. Every child at every age wants her parents to approve of her, to recognize what is special and unique about her, and to accept her for who she is. When we compare one child to the other, we pit them against each other, increasing their rivalry and making it harder for them to become friends.

Instead of saying something like, "Why don't you try out for the swim team as your sister did?" substitute, "Are there any after-school activities that sound fun to you?" If one child is a star, make special efforts to see what shines in your other child. Every person has a special talent. It just takes discovering and cultivating.

"Here's what I think about your marriage . . ."

"My parents have quite a weird relationship. Sometimes I look at them and they act so in love, like they are in high school or something. Then I see them fight and would swear that they hate each other. I suppose that's a good role model for relationships, though. It shows you have to stick together through all the ups and downs."
Age 13

Dr. Bassoff: There's a saying: "Happiness is not the absence of conflict but the ability to cope with it." That's what this girl is figuring out. Her parents, as she's discovering, are good role models. They're teaching her not the Hollywood version of love and marriage but

the down-to-earth one. This fortunate girl is learning that when her mom and dad are angry with each other, they eventually work through their problems. That is a good blueprint for her if she marries.

Of course, there are constructive and destructive ways to express anger. If you intentionally mock, insult, or humiliate your spouse or are physically abusive, you are modeling destructive behaviors. On the other hand, if you can counter your spouse without attacking his or her character and are able to air differences without devaluing opinions or feelings, you are teaching your daughter that confronting conflicts is safe and ultimately healing.

"My mother is stuck in a marriage where her husband treats her really badly. If she argues with him, he makes her feel stupid. It upsets me to see him treat her this way and get away with it. I will never let myself get in her situation. It's a miserable life, and she takes it out on her children."
Age unknown

Dr. Bassoff: It's hard to see your parents tear each other down. To her credit, this girl is set on not following her mother's example in her future relationships. However, she will have to be very conscientious about becoming different from her mother. After all, like it or not, parents are a child's most powerful role models. When you and your spouse treat each other respectfully, your daughter naturally expects—and models—this kind of behavior in her relationships. As many married couples know, it's possible to create a much better marriage than the one your parents had, but it takes a strong will.

"Here's how I feel about your divorce . . ."

"My parents are divorced, but they still like each other as friends. I'm happy with that. My dad does things like take my mom out to dinner with us for Mother's Day. I don't think all divorces turn out to be a big mess."
Age 13

Dr. Bassoff: A divorce is always traumatic for children because ultimately they want to be loved and cared for by both parents under the same roof. However, there are good and bad divorces. If your marriage ends, you can make your divorce healthy for your daughter by ensuring she can still

count on your emotional availability. Whatever your personal feelings are toward your ex-spouse, do not let them interfere with the job of parenting. The child's needs for care, support, and supervision always come first.

"My parents are divorced and they don't interact well at all. My dad is a mean person, and my mom is not very understanding. I have spoken to them about how their arguing makes me feel, and it doesn't help. Seeing how their relationship turned out, I know not to take abuse of any kind, and I know different characteristics to watch out for in a guy."
Age 14

Dr. Bassoff: In a bad divorce, the divorced parents remain more invested in their hostility toward each other than in the welfare of their child. If you use your daughter as a pawn or as a mediator, she will feel as if she is being torn in two.

The girl who wrote this letter is suffering. Her pain would be greatly reduced if her parents did not involve her in their conflicts and if they could sincerely assure her of their continuing love for her. If you face this struggle, try words

like these with your daughter:
"I know I am angry and impatient
a lot. I know I'm acting different
around you now, and that probably
scares you because you don't
know what to expect from me. The
divorce is taking a toll on me, but
please believe me when I say that
I love you as much as ever and will
try my best to once again become
the parent you can count on."

YOUR ROLE

Accept the paradox. One minute your daughter will turn to you for solace, and the next she'll push you away. This will be less confusing and hurtful if you remind yourself that she wants to be part of the family *and* she wants to be on her own.

Give her privacy. Make sure your daughter has a room with a door she can close. Before entering, always knock and ask, "May I come in?" Insist your other children respect their sister's privacy as well. Strong boundaries make for good family relationships.

Give her a diary. It's the best material gift you can give your daughter. You will be tempted to read it. Don't!

Moms, take heart. As your daughter pulls away from you, you will be freed up. Now is the time to do the things you put on hold when she was younger. Cultivate your talents and dreams, just as your daughter is doing. This is one way she can be your role model.

Dads, she needs you. In adolescence, your daughter needs you more than ever before. Teach her skills that will prepare her for the world, from how to change a tire to how to tell a joke.

Strengthen your marriage. During your child's tumultuous teen years, your marriage may become stressed. Fortify it. Go on weekly dates with your spouse. Get away for a romantic weekend every two months. Make your sex life a priority again.

Strengthen family ties. Initiate activities that draw family members together. Camp, create holiday traditions, play games, and volunteer for community projects.

Expect your daughter to contribute to the household. Agree on chores that will challenge her and promote her competence, such as cooking a weekly meal for the family or mowing the lawn.

If you divorce, strengthen the connection to your child. Girls with divorced parents need their parents' support, care, and supervision more than ever before. If you are too stressed to carry out all your parental responsibilities, enlist other loving and responsible adults who can be there for her.

Be kind to your ex-spouse. If you are divorced, make a point of frequently saying something positive about your former spouse to your daughter. Remember that she identifies with both of you.

If you are remarried, have realistic expectations. Just because you love both your new spouse and your daughter doesn't mean they'll love each other. Expect instead mutual kindness and respect.

Problems shared are problems halved. Talk openly with your daughter about the tensions and frustrations that everyone in the new family is feeling. Show her that you and your new spouse recognize her feelings.

CHAPTER

Friends Forever?

by Virginia Beane Rutter, M.S.

"My friends are drifting away, and it's killing me. It hurts to sit alone at lunch and have no one speak to me. I feel completely invisible. I wish I could believe other people just don't see me, but they do. I know they are rejecting me because of my outside image. They don't see my heart and mind. Everyone thinks I can handle it, but inside, part of me is dying."

Age 13

During your daughter's preteen and teenage years, her friendships can be so deeply emotional that they seem to eclipse everything else in her life. Friends are utterly important in adolescence, yet, for some girls, making friends can seem an insurmountable task. Girl groups are rife with friction, envy, jealousy, competitiveness, and exclusiveness. At the same time, such groups provide the social laboratory, security, and stimulation girls need to mature.

In early elementary school, girls' friendships are transitional and flexible. Girls "try on" different kinds of friends and learn how to relate to various people around them. As they grow older, girls become more selective, choosing fewer girls to spend time with and getting to know them better. Best friends become more important. In these tight relationships, girls learn about another person in depth. Intense friendships are an early form of an intimate relationship with someone outside a girl's family.

It is in fifth or sixth grade that cliques really develop among girls. Having a group of friends is of key importance to your daughter's middle-school and high-school life. Without friends, a girl can fall into a dark abyss; she can feel invisible. Sometimes a girl just "disappears" in her social milieu—no one says "hello" anymore, asks her questions, or calls out her name on the school grounds. The girl whose letter opens this chapter has suffered this powerful rejection, and it has seriously diminished her self-esteem. The more invisible she feels, the more she withdraws. Feeling inadequate, she is afraid to reach out and be ridiculed even more. She knows she is being judged on her image, not on her "heart and mind," but that knowledge alone can't help her break the spell she has fallen under.

When She's Alone

Be alert to what is happening between your daughter and her friends. Pay attention to whether the phone rings and to the way she talks about other people. If she seems depressed, no one calls for her, and she doesn't talk about other girls or go out with friends, then she may be in trouble. But don't try to push your daughter into a mold. A 10-year-old may be content with her family. A 14-year-old is usually desperate for a close circle of friends, but some older girls are slow to mature. At any age, a girl often reverts to the family when there has been a trauma at school or home, or even after she makes a big developmental leap. An accident, the death of a parent or classmate, or a month away doing community service are only a few situations that may prompt a girl to stay close to home for a while. After such a significant event, your daughter may need the touchstone of security that you provide in order to regroup.

The girl who wrote our opening letter needs some assistance from the adults around her. She feels intense pain and is shriveling up inside. If no one intervenes to help her find new ways of dealing with her social woes, her self-diminishment could affect other areas of her life. Her mother or father should size up the situation as objectively as they can. If she talks about a tragic social faux pas yet is still surrounded by friends, she may be exaggerating her scenario. But this girl is expressing an all-too-real teenage despair that needs to be addressed. Her parents need to approach her with compassion, saying, "We can see you are hurting. What can we do to help?"

If your daughter experiences intense isolation, take her seriously. Social rejection is a source of great anxiety for girls. It can undermine their confidence in their ability to master new situations. In its extreme, it can lead to unhealthy behaviors and patterns, such as having unprotected sex and substance abuse. It is not as common that a group of girls will outright reject one of their friends as it is that a girl might be gradually pushed away, ostracized, or forced out. But the easy advice—walk away and look for friendship elsewhere—is not easy to follow. Your daughter may be so crushed that she withdraws instead of making overtures to other girls. Help her as she takes time to recover. Meanwhile, encourage her to find activities in which she will naturally meet new friends.

> *"Last week a girl was mad at me, and she turned everyone else against me. Then all of a sudden these girls decided I was their friend again. I know it's not healthy to stay friends with them."*
> Age 14

Like Mother, Like Daughter

To remember just how important friends are to your daughter, think back to your own early adolescent years. Mothers, remember the intense bond you had with your girlfriends. As your daughter separates from you, her questions about her female relationships may stir up similar questions for you. Her changes can thrust you into a reexamination of your own coming-of-age, which can be uncomfortable. Pay attention to the strong feelings that may well up inside you—they will help you identify your own conflicts and see how your experiences influence the responses you give your daughter. You may see yourself through her eyes or hear echoes of the arguments you had with your mother. This is an opportunity to gain self-knowledge and avoid the kind of impasse you may have had with your own parents.

Remember the times when you were in black despair, feeling isolated, angry, awkward, or abandoned when a friend rejected you. Thinking about when you felt out of the group will help you have compassion when your daughter hits difficult times. Try not to shrug off

"I don't have many friends. People make fun of me because I'm overweight and I do well in school, which others think is not cool. They call me 'Brains' and 'Four Eyes.' Last year I cried every day about it, and sometimes I still cry."
age 11

her pain with comments like, "It's not a big deal," or "Stop overreacting." Remembering your own hurt will help you give her the understanding she needs.

If you are haunted by a teenage experience of feeling left out, you may feel elated when your daughter includes you and asks you to drive a group of girls to a basketball game. But don't try to become "one of the girls"; your daughter still wants you to be her parent. You can't redo your own adolescence by living through your daughter and her friends. But the wonderful secret is this: if you are reconciling your past with your current values, understanding your own daughter helps you understand yourself in a new way. And you can heal some of your wounds by using what you learned as an adolescent to mother your daughter as she runs this gauntlet.

Know Her Friends' World

Recalling your own adolescence is helpful, but clearly things have changed since you were your daughter's age. Use her girlfriends to measure some of the behavior you may find questionable. You may find that tank tops with bra straps showing are an ordinary fashion statement, for instance, while in your day they may have been scandalous. Ask nonjudgmental questions about issues that startle you in your daughter's behavior, dress, or language. Rather than trying to control her, this spirit of inquiry should support your connection with her. It also is smart to get to know a few of her girlfriends' parents well enough to check with them now and then about what is going on with your daughter. Your teenager may object to parents who collaborate this way, but in the end it can be beneficial to your relationship.

On a deeper level, your daughter's relationships with other girls serve to mirror and amplify her own femininity. Mothers, just as you were the original mirror for her femaleness, now other feminine influences become important. Although your daughter will continue to need you to model womanhood, she must have interplay with other girls to find her own identity. Your warm connection with her will help her be a good friend to other girls.

You can continue to be the role model for your daughter's relationships with her girlfriends. Who are your good female friends?

What are your relationships with them like? Your daughter wants to see that women friends have a place in your life. She, too, will build female support systems that will hold her through the difficult times in her life. As she solidifies these relationships, she will go back and forth between you and them. Each relationship enhances the other.

Girl Friends and Guy Friends

It is vital for your daughter to find at least one intimate girlfriend to count on in middle school and high school. Studies have shown that girls work more productively and effectively with one another; they cooperate on homework, in team sports, and in the classroom. Girls are enlivened by this kind of creative collaboration.

But in the friendships and cliques that develop, there is often an underlying competition for thinness, beauty, or attention from boys. This competition can get in the way of girls finding friends in whom they can truly trust. Just as girls have radar for their mother's weak points, they also scan for other girls' weaknesses.

"I have a friend who's perfect. She always gets straight As, she has a great family, great looks, and a super life. The bad thing is she brags about it. Sometimes I'm envious of her always being the most popular, the prettiest, and the best at everything!"
Age 11

A girl who has too high an opinion of herself or who has a characteristic that other girls find irritating will very quickly find those girls putting her down.

Adolescent girls and boys often develop deep nonsexual friendships. They talk to each other not only about their fears, joys, successes, and failures, but also about everything from algebra homework to family problems. Sifting through emotional issues and social conflicts in a group of boys and girls helps your daughter learn to negotiate intimate relationships. True friendships with boys form the basis of healthy dating or intimate relationships.

Family and Friends

If your daughter has problems with her friends, she may yearn to withdraw from them and cling to you. But it is important that she find her own community. You can encourage her to stay in touch with a strong sense of self by reinforcing activities she loves to do. If she follows her passions in spite of being pulled this way and that by friends, she will stay on course. You will have to walk a fine line between allowing her to choose her own friends and being aware of who they are and what they are up to. Be observant and neutral. If you are reactive, she will hide herself and her friendships from you.

If she complains about one of her friends, don't jump on the bandwagon with your own criticisms. By the next day, they may be bosom buddies again. Take what your daughter shares as only one reality; it may reflect the current state of her friendship rather than a reliable character assessment of her friend. Also remember that if you always see your daughter as innocent and her friends as the bad influence, she will take her friends' side and turn away. If, over time, you get clues that her friends are up to no good, then you'll need to intervene.

You can foster your daughter's friendships by making your home a welcoming place for her girlfriends. If she asks you to make dinner for them, enjoy it; bask in the girls' exuberance. Encourage their interests and enjoyment of each other. Being the accommodating driver for movies or jobs and even picking them up from parties will earn you your daughter's goodwill.

You will be mostly a spectator in these events, but you will stay connected to your daughter.

Honor your daughter's capacity to be both vulnerable and self-sufficient. Balance her developing independence with her need for you. If you do that, she will be able to form friendships with other girls and women in which she can express herself fully, see herself mirrored, and grow.

Virginia Beane Rutter is a mother, teacher, and author of **Celebrating Girls: Nurturing and Empowering Our Daughters** *and* **Embracing Persephone: How to Be the Mother You Want for the Daughter You Cherish.** *She is a practicing marriage and family therapist and certified Jungian analyst specializing in feminine psychology.*

LISTENING IN

Virginia Beane Rutter explores girls' questions about the good and bad sides of close friendships.

"My friendships are *so* important."
"I can tell my friends everything and know they won't tell others. We can play stupid games or do anything together. If you look ugly or act stupid, they're the types who won't care. I feel cool around my friends. Without them, I'd lead a lonely and terrible life."
Age 11
Ms. Beane Rutter: This girl "feels cool" around her friends. What she means, I think, is "comfortable." These friends have established a level of trust that allows her to express herself fully and spontaneously without fear of ridicule. Not having to be on her guard is one of the primary reasons she is grateful for her friends. Your daughter needs strong friendships with other girls in order to be comfortable with herself.

This girl also can trust her friends not to betray her confidences. Trust and betrayal are frequent themes in girls' relationships and often come up when a relationship between two girls ends. If your daughter fears she has told her friend her whole life story and now the friend has betrayed her by telling her secrets, acknowledge that this makes her feel fragile and vulnerable. Over time she will be more careful about how much of herself she wants to share.

"My friends make me experience all kinds of emotions: sometimes they cheer me up and other times they even make me mad. But I can always talk to my friends."
Age 14
Ms. Beane Rutter: Girls learn about the complexities of relationships through their friends. They continually mull over, describe, and analyze the personalities of other girls in their group. Most of this happens on the phone or at sleepovers with friends. Through intense analysis of one another, girls become more self-aware. This girl recognizes the extreme feelings that arise in her friendships—both joy and anger. She doesn't expect her relationships to be one-dimensional.

Riding the fierce emotional waves of friendships is good practice for your daughter in negotiating her mature relationships with women. In all the back and forth, push and pull of affection and rejection, she learns what is real friendship and what she can count on. As a parent, your job is to stay in the background and be the relationship she can count on to be stable through all her changes.

"I don't fit in."

I'm shy, so I don't have many friends. When the kids in my class choose partners, no one picks me. I have glasses, curly hair, and a stupid last name. I try to fit in, and I always have the latest styles, like butterfly clips for my hair. Why doesn't anyone like me? I don't have a clue.
Age 10

Ms. Beane Rutter: Ten years old is often a painfully shy time for a girl. The good news is that your daughter is still young enough to confide in you about feeling left out. By age 15, she is more likely to keep it to herself or balk at your "interference." But this girl is asking for help.

If your daughter picks herself apart looking for clues as to why kids don't like her, listen with empathy and say, "I'm so sorry for how badly you feel. But the real issue isn't your last name or your looks. Kids are trying to stake out a place in the social group, and sometimes they do it by making fun of others. Trust me, things will change as you get older. You will be more valued for your intelligence. Meanwhile, let's talk about what you can do to make friends now."

Just hearing the emotional truth of the situation from a loving adult is reassuring to a girl. Problem solve by offering suggestions, such as that she invite the friends she does have over more often. Focusing her attention on one other sympathetic girl may be life saving. Teach your daughter to be the one doing the choosing when she has to pick a partner. Role-play who she would ask and how; she can be shy and still be empowered. Give her books with female protagonists who are going through similarly humiliating times with friends. Suggestions: *Because of Winn-Dixie* by Kate DiCamillo (a new girl in town makes friends with the help of her unusual dog); *All Alone in the Universe* by Lynne Rae Perkins (a longtime friendship crumbles);

and *The Secret Voice of Gina Zhang* by Dori Jones Yang (a girl makes a friend in spite of her shyness).

"Yesterday I was sitting in class not saying a word and my classmate said, 'You never talk. You're so weird.' I have friends, but I don't really talk to many people because I'm afraid of being rejected. I'm quiet, but I don't seem to just blend in. I know I have friends, but when I'm around other people who are talking and having a good time and I'm just sitting there, I feel terrible. I think it is difficult to make friends, because most people in middle and high school are in their cliques and not interested in letting you join."
Age 13

Ms. Beane Rutter: These years can be excruciatingly embarrassing, awkward, and confusing for girls. All your daughter's lovable personality traits will now come under intense scrutiny from her peers. She will constantly be challenged, often in cruel ways, on every point of her behavior and character.

Middle-school and high-school girls are clique-oriented and exclusionary. This girl feels the pressure of being on the fringe of the estab-lished groups. She has an intro-verted personality that becomes suspect in the extroverted world of teen life. Rather than getting stuck on the fact that she's not saying anything, help her focus on becoming an active listener to the others "who are talking and having a good time." Shy or not, be sure that your daughter is involved in a physical activity, whether it be a team sport or an individual compe-tition or discipline. Challenging herself physically has been proven to give a girl self-confidence that translates to better mastery of emotional skills.

"I feel so lonely."
"Last year my two best friends were always there for me in tough situa-tions. This year we are in separate classes, so it's harder to see each other. They both found new friends. I try to communicate with them, but it doesn't work. I try to make other friends, but it's not the same. It makes me very sad."
Age unknown

Ms. Beane Rutter: "Out of sight, out of mind" is, unfortunately, true for friendships. Losing friends through circumstance can be just as hurtful to a girl as rejection. Never underestimate or discount

the impact of such a loss on your daughter. Her grief can lower her self-esteem, impinge on her life performance, or, in extreme cases, lead to depression.

Depending on her age, if your daughter is in a situation like this, you will need to be there for her in different ways. A young girl will welcome her parent's company after such a loss. It is more difficult with an older girl, because neither your input nor your presence can completely solve the problem. Listening and sympathizing can help, but steer clear of dismissive comments such as, "Oh, cheer up," or "Don't be silly, you'll find other friends." Girls have been known to change high schools rather than face a hostile peer group, and often they succeed socially in a new school. If you notice that your daughter is crying a lot in her room, losing her appetite or gaining weight excessively, or performing poorly in school, try to get to the bottom of what is troubling her. If you feel it is over your head and hers, get help from a professional.

"I feel lonely a lot, but I like it. I enjoy spending time with myself, but I do have times when I wish

I knew more people. It's not that I don't fit in with others. I feel they don't fit in with me."
Age 14

Ms. Beane Rutter: As she matures, a girl begins to develop a sense of proportion about friends. Her social group is primary, but she also values herself as an individual. This girl is already enjoying time alone. The age at which girls appreciate time alone varies dramatically. More introverted girls (or girls from more introspective families) may have already discovered joy in aloneness as young children. Others may be well into adulthood before they can appreciate the gift of time to themselves. A balance between aloneness and connection is the goal. This girl has developed a strong sense of self, so strong that she is finding it difficult to meet others who match her. Her individuality is progressing nicely, but she also needs to develop her social skills and interactions.

If your daughter feels this way, she may need more interaction with her peers or, if she is too mature for them, she may have to wait until college for things to equal out so that she can develop friendships with other women.

Girls who are unusually sophisticated, emotionally or intellect-
ually, sometimes just can't relate
to the teenage world.

"My friend has it all."
*"I am envious of one of my friends.
She is popular, and good-looking
guys ask her out. She is really thin.
(I am thin, too, though.) She has
beautiful hair and the coolest
clothes. (I have cool clothes, too,
but she has more.) I sometimes
try to look and act like her, but
then I realize that being myself
is okay."*
Age 12

Ms. Beane Rutter: If you find your
daughter struggling to be a look-
alike of a girlfriend, gently intervene to see if you can get her to
recognize her own good qualities.
Is she focusing on superficialities
to the exclusion of deeper qualities
of integrity, loyalty, and caring?
Ask yourself where she is getting
these values. Do you obsess about
your weight? Do you place a high
value on material possessions?
Be willing to ask yourself tough
questions, but don't blame yourself. Give yourself credit for recognizing your own shadow. Then ask
yourself how both you and your
daughter can turn things around.

*"Last year I had two friends who
weren't friends with each other.
This year, they're suddenly calling
each other every other day, planning their wardrobes together,
going to the movies on Friday
night, and leaving me out of all of
it. I'm jealous, and I told one girl
I felt left out. She told me not to
worry about it because it would
hurt our friendship. All I could
think was, 'What friendship?' "*
Age 13

**Ms. Beane Rutter: Painful friend-
ship** triangles among girls begin
as early as preschool. Back then
when trouble hit, your daughter
could find refuge with you, but
now she has to make new friends.
Being able to talk to you, though,
will give her the courage to reenter
the fray. When you are confronted
with your daughter's distress,
listen and empathize. Tell her
about a time you were in a similar
plight. Your sympathetic ear and
insights about the nature of jealousy and friendships will help her
work it out and prepare for future
disappointments. Then try to
explore her relationship with her
friends. What might have led up
to the alienation? Don't blame
her for the break, but help her to
look at both sides.

Help her feel secure enough to endure a temporary separation from her friends. While even a week is a long time for a teenager, you can offer a longer perspective. If she spends time with other girls, her friends may come around at some point. If the split becomes permanent, you will want her to realize after the initial disappointment that the rejection is not a reflection of her worth but part of the ebb and flow of relationships. Someday when she is in the position of power, of rejecting or demeaning another girl, perhaps she will be able to handle the situation in a less hurtful manner.

"My friend can be really mean."

"My best friend hits me and puts me down, but when I tell her to stop she gets mad. I feel like I'm being tortured, and I'm tired of it."
Age unknown

Ms. Beane Rutter: The high pitch of girls' relationships can result in physical abuse and bullying. This girl is confused—she is still calling the other girl her "best friend" although she feels "tortured" by her. The girl in power here is controlling the weaker girl with her anger and exploitation. One good sign is that our letter writer is "tired of it," which shows not only that she might accept intervention but also that she may be developing the strength to seek more wholesome relationships.

Parents should intervene to stop abuse in relationships. If your daughter complains of such behavior, you need to talk to her seriously and consistently to help her define what is a healthy relationship. Don't forbid her to see her friend, but work with her on having more self-respect and on setting limits that don't include abusive behavior. If her friend still treats her badly, gradually help her wean herself from the friendship. You don't want her to begin a repetitive cycle of relationships in which she is maltreated.

"Girls get involved in gossiping about people. It's mean and it hurts. Yet I have to admit I've gossiped about people, too. I have also been the object of gossip. Once someone started a rumor that I had done sexual things with one of my ex-boyfriends. It made me feel awful, because I'm saving myself for marriage. After that I haven't really had much interest in dating."
Age 14

Ms. Beane Rutter: Gossiping is another medium through which girls negotiate their social scenes. Teenagers use it constantly to process their relationships. This girl admits that she has also gossiped and that she has been the recipient of some untruths. But she is going too far in withdrawing from her own life and giving up dating in order to avoid having people talk about her. Instead of changing her behavior on the basis of unfounded rumors, she needs to focus on her own truth and realize that people will talk about her, or not, whatever she does or doesn't do.

Teach your daughter to grow a thick skin when she gets wind of idle talk. She can do only what feels right to her. She can't please the entire public. If she has good friends, she can deny untrue allegations and convey her own values without having to withdraw because of others' loose tongues.

"We're always fighting."

"This girl and I had a huge fight for almost two years. It started with just the two of us but ended up with a lot of people taking sides. There was hair pulling, yelling, and name-calling. I went home in tears almost every day. Finally this girl and I got sent to the principal's office—otherwise it probably would have lasted longer."
Age 11

Ms. Beane Rutter: If your daughter comes home in tears frequently, something is wrong! Get to the bottom of it as gently and tactfully as you can. Say, "I can see you're troubled, honey. Tell me about it. Let's see if there's anything to be done. I won't do anything without telling you first." This way you assure her that you won't impulsively rush in and make things worse.

When a girl is 11 years old, it is definitely appropriate for a parent to call the principal when a situation is extreme. Even teens are glad that adults set limits when something beyond their control is happening with peers. If your daughter talks to you but resists your intervening because she is afraid of being branded a tattletale or a baby, assess for yourself whether or not to override her worries. If you do go against her wishes, tell her you need to alert the school authorities out of concern for her and other students, and assure her that you will be as discreet about it as possible.

"My friends may be in trouble."

"My parents thought I was hanging around with a bad crowd, and we fought about it a lot. I explained that I still act the same way I did before I made those friends. I told my parents I'm the one making choices about what I do. My friends don't make those choices for me. I am my own person."

Age 14

Ms. Beane Rutter: This girl is asserting her rights to choose her friends without her parents' influence and to make decisions about her behavior without her friends' influence. Making her own choices is a dramatic issue in adolescence. This girl's parents are pressuring her so much that their conflict may push her into rebelling. That would destroy the balance she is trying to establish: being centered in her own values in spite of being pulled by her friends one way and by her parents another.

If you worry about your daughter's friends, observe her behavior for a while to see if there is anything to be alarmed about. If you smell smoke on her or her friends' clothes, for example, bring it up in an unloaded way. Say something like, "Amy has a strong smoky odor about her. I wonder what you think about that." No matter what she says, emphasize simply your concern about her health.

If you discover, however, that her friends are driving drunk, stealing, or doing other dangerous things, you must intervene. Assume your daughter is somehow also involved, however peripherally. If you see your daughter as the angel and blame her friends, she will take their side against you. Have a long talk about her association with these friends and her behavior. Why is she hanging out with them? What's in it for her?

Make your rules and values clear. Focus on her safety and the privileges she enjoys based on her not participating in dangerous or illegal behaviors. Don't get hung up on the refrain, "You lied to me." Talk about mutual trust. You can't influence her friends, but you do have an influence on her. Through ongoing conversation in which she feels your love and concern, she can be empowered to make healthier choices.

"My friend told me her father hits her a lot for no reason. She has begun to date already when most of us haven't. She says dating makes her feel wanted and loved.

Recently, she started to take the drug acid. She says it makes her feel better, but she does weird things when she takes it. It's beginning to scare me and I'm worried. I don't know what to do."
Age unknown

Ms. Beane Rutter: A teenage girl sometimes finds herself friends with another girl whose problems are out of her league. This girl's troubled friend tells her about a variety of serious problems, and our letter writer is rightly at a loss to know what to do to help. Hopefully she will tell her parents, and they will enable her to consult the school counselor, a sympathetic teacher, or the principal.

If your daughter finds herself in a friendship like this, praise her for her empathy and compassion, and make it clear that it's not her responsibility to take care of it on her own. Tell her, "It's good you came to me with this, because it is something adults and professionals have to address. Nothing you can do will help your friend change. Do you want to go to the teacher by yourself or shall we go together?"

Your daughter is not equipped to handle a friend's problems with drugs, alcohol, or sex; severe family problems; or mental illness. If the other girl gets professional help and doesn't go on draining your daughter, they can still be friends. But if it is still overwhelming to your daughter, you will have to help her set good limits on the relationship. Say, "Your friend's problems are causing you too much stress. By listening to all her problems, you may actually prevent her from seeking the help she needs. Let's talk about how you can limit your time with her and still be compassionate." This is healthy learning that will help her conduct wholesome relationships in the future.

"I have friends on the Internet."
"I have a lot of online friends. Some are close, and some are just casual chatters. Sometimes I feel more comfortable with my online friends because the screen separates us. I can tell them my true feelings without being afraid they'll tell someone at my school. At times I feel closer to people online than in real life, and that can hurt. It's like I don't have a real life— I'm a cybergirl."
Age 12

Ms. Beane Rutter: The Internet is a marvelous tool for learning and communicating. This girl says she can express her true feelings on the Web and trusts they won't come back to her at school. (The Internet has saved gay teenagers a lot of heartache by letting them come out in a safe way.) The Internet can also be enlightening if your daughter is using a site like The Diary Project (www.diaryproject.com), a chat room for kids ages 13 and older that offers places to write about relationships, drugs, friends, family, racism, and stress. Sites like these are intentionally therapeutic and can relieve the isolation some girls feel.

It is worrisome, however, that this girl is substituting virtual life for real life. The danger is that as she becomes more addicted to cyberspace, she will become less versed at "real" social skills. As with any activity, the key here is balance. Keep an eye on how much time your daughter is spending on the Internet and with whom. Does she also have an active social life? If she has access to both worlds, most girls prefer reality to fantasy. Be aware of what your daughter is doing,

and talk to her in a loving way about the issues.

"Online friendships are risky. The other person may lie and say he is 14 years old when in reality he is 40. People online find out your interests and can act like they agree with what you say. You may feel like the other person understands you, but he or she could be lying. People you see every day can lie to you, but not about their identity. Friends online may really be enemies."
Age 14

Ms. Beane Rutter: This girl understands a very real negative aspect of the Internet: she can be taken advantage of. She is right to distrust the truth of such relationships. In addition, the pornographic sites and unregulated communication on the Internet may expose her to information that is inappropriate for her age. Girls who stumble unwittingly on such sites may be in over their heads before they even realize what's happened.

Know what Web sites your daughter is visiting and how often. Be actively involved—look at sites with her and talk about what you see. Check out the chat rooms she likes; those monitored by systems operators can be safer than unmonitored forums, but they're not foolproof. You can also purchase software that blocks sites focusing on topics you choose to avoid.

Trust your instinct. If you're concerned about your daughter's Internet use, don't be impulsive and accuse her out of hand. Be considerate about your approach, and you will win her trust.

YOUR ROLE

Expect heartache. When your daughter moves from grammar school to middle school to high school, expect her idyllic girlhood friendships to be disrupted.

Pay attention to her cues. Expect her friendships to change daily, and check out the current status before you comment on anything. Otherwise you may get pushed away for not understanding.

Be part of the solution. Strive not to get overinvolved. Keep some detachment so that you can be objective when she needs you.

Moms, how do you talk about your girlfriends? Are you giving her the right messages? Stay away from competitiveness or put-downs. She learns from your actions.

Dads, how do you treat her friends? Stay allied with her by respecting her and her friends. Do not comment on her girlfriends' bodies (or your daughter's body, either).

Don't criticize her friends. If you do, you'll face a closed door. Try to remain neutral as all the chaos swirls around you.

Beware of boundaries. Your daughter will not want you to compete for her friends' time and attention. Let her be with her peers. But be available to spend time with her when she needs you.

Change her scene. If your daughter is miserable with her social group, help her get out of her normal environment by going to camp or joining an activity. If she can make one or two friends outside school, she'll feel better about herself.

Ask for help. If your daughter is continually ostracized or cruelly teased, seek counseling for her. If she thinks her only option is to tough it out, she may be in over her head before you are aware of it.

School and Sports

by JoAnn Deak, Ph.D.

"I'm really nervous about starting middle school. I'm afraid
I won't know kids in my classes and that I'll be the worst in every
subject, including gym. You have to change classrooms, and I'm
afraid my locker will be so far away that I'll always be late. What
if my locker isn't near my friends'? Everyone else seems calm about
middle school, but I mostly feel afraid. Do you think I'm normal?
For all I know, I could be insane."

age 11

I n your daughter's life, school is an incubator for all things
exciting, promising, fulfilling, doubt-provoking, and sometimes
frightening. It is *her* world, where she must step away from your
protective arms and make it on her own. She has to speak out, prove
herself, and be graded on it to boot. Every day is an exercise, not
just in stretching and strengthening her mind, but also in negotiating the social and political circles of her peers. Similarly, the
athletic fields and courts your daughter treads offer stimulating
challenges and potential minefields, as she learns to compete
against and work with her peers, strive for goals, and discover how
deeply her inner desires for independence and success run.

The girl whose letter opens this chapter has just come face-to-
face with one of young girls' predominant schooltime concerns:
she is frazzled and fearful about middle school. What she doesn't

know is that while other girls may appear to her to be unworried, gliding like ducks on the surface of a smooth pond, underwater they are *all* paddling like mad.

Meeting New Challenges

For girls, the change from elementary school to middle school is a harsh adjustment. Part of it has to do with the "structure" of elementary and middle schools and the "structure" of girls. Connections with others are the cornerstone of life for females, and young girls have close relationships with their teachers and classmates. The self-contained classes of the primary grades, with one homeroom teacher and the same classmates all day, feel predictable and safe. For some girls, middle school feels like an incredible number of changes each day. Elementary school is like those comfortable old sneakers that are broken in just the way you like them. Middle school is like a new shoe that pinches all over.

> *"I'm not a bad student, but this year I had trouble adjusting to fifth grade. I forgot my homework twice and almost missed two major projects. I'm doing better now, but I can't stop worrying about my schoolwork."*
>
> Age 11

You can help your daughter with the transition by empathizing with her worries and letting her know you have faith in her. If she feels overwhelmed, try, "You're right. There is a lot to manage and get used to this year. But I know that with some planning, you can do it." Help her organize her time. Assist her in setting a schedule for doing homework after school. Keep an eye on her long-term projects and help her break them down into reasonable goals with deadlines. Check how her work is going, but do not take responsibility for getting it done. You can model good work habits, too: while she studies, do your own work or pay bills.

Fading Interest

As your daughter advances in school, the increasing challenges of her classwork can lead to another situation parents often notice: their daughter who used to love school has become disenchanted or less interested in it. Academically, some girls sail through the transition to tougher schoolwork, increased homework, and a new class structure. But it is not uncommon for some girls who used to get everything right on the Friday spelling test in the primary grades to find middle school less understandable, more demanding, and less fun.

What happened? First, there is the social pressure. Girls often walk a tightrope of appearing smart, but not too smart, so they will fit in. Some continue to get good grades but do it more covertly, participating less vocally and visibly in class.

> *"People in my classes call me brainy and make fun of me. Then they take advantage of me, calling me at night to get answers to their homework. It is so unfair, because they are overpowering and I'm too shy to say no."*
>
> Age 13

A conceptual shift also happens between the elementary and middle-school years. The elementary years are designed for "learning to" skills: learning to read, learning to write, and learning to calculate. In middle school, there is a rather dramatic shift to "application skills"—girls are now applying what they learned during their elementary education. They are no longer learning to read; they are reading to learn. They are writing to express their thoughts and calculating to problem solve.

To an adult this shift may sound minor, but to a young person it is a huge leap. "Learning to" thinking is sequential, detailed, and exact. Applying those skills requires more complex thinking that is not always sequential. Often there are many ways of doing the same task.

If your daughter's interest in school has waned, talk with her teachers and guidance counselor about what your daughter is like in class. They may see a different girl than you do. Have they noticed her getting distracted or seen other reasons for her discouragement? Solicit their support. Ask your daughter if she'd like you to set up an adult contact for her at school. Having one adult she knows she can talk to when she feels lost can help.

Staying close by when she does her homework can also help. If you sit with her when she studies, she will feel like she is not alone, even if you are reading a novel or balancing your checkbook. If everything at school feels different and difficult, your presence while she does homework can provide familiarity and physical stability. It says, "I am going to be here with you."

Celebrate the present and get excited about the future. When she has finished a big project, brought home good grades, or given a nerve-wracking oral report, order pizza and rent a movie to celebrate. If your daughter is in eighth or ninth grade, take her to visit college campuses and show her all that the schools offer—socially and culturally as well as academically. Connect her with professionals in fields she is interested in and talk about what educational background those jobs require.

On the Athletic Field

A recently published major study stated that girls who participate in sports succeed better in school, have better physical and mental health, and learn valuable problem-solving and leadership skills.[1] Sports can make your daughter feel strong and confident. If she thinks of herself as a runner or a rock climber, she feels powerful,

1. Jean Zimmerman and Gil Reavill, *Raising Our Athletic Daughters* (New York: Doubleday, 1998).

competent, and part of a world of athletes—even if she does not compete as part of a team. She defines herself as a person who can accomplish things. That confidence will spill over into activities off the field.

When you support your daughter's participation in sports, you are investing in her future. It is important for girls to learn how to handle competition effectively, and sports is one of the best ways to do that. Your encouragement during her preteen years is important, because the typical girl becomes less active during adolescence. The elementary or middle-school years are a good time to get your daughter involved in sports, because the competition can be less intense than in high school.

> *"My family supports me in my favorite sport: horseback riding. They are also positive about the other sports I play: softball, volleyball, swimming, and diving. Doing well in sports makes me feel proud of myself. I feel good when people compliment me on my talents, attitude, or ability. I feel proud when I excel in my sports or when my horses and I do well at shows."*
> Age 13

Some girls have personalities and temperaments that are better suited to individual activities such as track or tennis rather than a team sport. If your daughter balks at organized sports, help her find more unconventional activities that can get her heart pumping. There doesn't need to be a scoreboard for the sport to be beneficial to her. How about canoeing, yoga, wilderness hiking, or snowshoeing? Fitness walking is a great habit to get into, and if you walk alongside your daughter, it can also be a time to talk.

> *"I get stressed out during dance competitions. If you make one mistake, the whole team hates you and talks behind your back. It's bad enough that they make fun of you, but thinking about it can make you so tense you can't dance. That gets you in bigger trouble."*
> Age 12

Dealing with Competition

We want our daughters to have the inner drive that compels them
to strive to be the best they can be—in school or sports—and to
feel that sense of pride and satisfaction that comes from giving
their best. We also want them to experience loss and learn how
to be resilient.

Yet it is important to understand that the drive to excel is somewhat related to temperament. Some girls are driven to perform
and compete in academics and
sports, whereas others are happier
with noncompetitive activities. A
highly competitive parent and a laid-
back child can be a tough combination. Although we can encourage
children to try hard and to do a good
job, we cannot teach them to have a
burning competitive drive. It just
doesn't work that way.

*"I am extremely competitive! No
one causes me to be that way; I do
it myself. In school, I always try to
get the highest grades. When I'm
in a play, I always press myself to
make the most of my character.
I try to play the hardest and do my
best in sports, too."*
age 13

If your daughter consistently shies away from sports competition or seems threatened by how she stacks up against peers in
the classroom, gently try to find out what is holding her back. If
she makes generalizations such as "I'm just not competitive" or
"I don't like sports," she may be covering up feelings of incompe-
tence, anxiousness about participating in a public arena, or fear
of failure. Build her confidence by starting her off with small hur-
dles. Break down intimidating sports skills into easier, practicable
steps. Play games that build her coordination at home; tossing
the Frisbee, playing catch, or casually shooting hoops in the drive-
way will increase her comfort level with her body and improve
her hand-eye coordination without public scrutiny. Getting her

involved in a performance-based activity, such as music or public speaking, can help her feel more confident in the classroom.

Finding a Balance

So, let's check our list: You are supposed to help your daughter focus on her homework, participate in sports, *and* make her mark in extracurricular activities. That sounds like a pretty full plate. How do you keep your daughter from being overscheduled?

I like to think of making choices about activities, lessons, and sports as being like visiting a smorgasbord. The first few times you visit, you tend to take many different things in smaller quantities so that you can taste them all. As time goes by, you gradually taste all the items you fancy until, finally, you become more selective, choosing only a few foods but in greater quantity.

In elementary school, provide your daughter with a number of choices to explore. Let her sample interests, and don't apply too much pressure if her passion for certain pursuits waxes and wanes. She is experimenting. By the time she reaches middle school, her interests will be narrowing down. She may want to eliminate some activities to focus on others. You can provide her with balance so that she gets what she needs: praise for her accomplishments, support when she is in distress, and faith that you will be there for her either way.

Dr. JoAnn Deak has been a teacher, school psychologist, counselor in private practice, and administrator. She is author of **How Girls Thrive: An Essential Guide for Educators (and Parents)**, *is co-editor of* **The Book of Hopes and Dreams for Girls and Young Women,** *and is currently working on a book entitled* **Knowing Girls, Growing Girls.** *She is founder of The DEAK Group, a consulting service for schools and parents.*

LISTENING IN

Dr. Deak looks at how girls can achieve and compete at their best—in the classroom and on the playing field.

"I don't like school anymore."

"Until I started fifth grade, I had always done well in school. It's so hard now. I've started to get Cs in some of my classes. My parents say that's not acceptable, and I feel stupid."

Age 10

Dr. Deak: This scenario is not rare. It sounds as if this girl's grades are not due to slacking off or an uncaring attitude. She clearly cares about how she fares academically. If your daughter has a similar struggle, spend some time figuring out what would help her do better in her classes. Listen to what she thinks is going on, and talk to her teachers to get a better perspective. Your goal is to find out where she feels the biggest struggles are: is it in a particular subject, or is she in a time crunch? Nagging and threatening her will not be effective at this point, because she already feels like a failure; what she really needs is to know that you love and support her.

"My teacher doesn't like me."

"My teacher snaps at kids sometimes. It hurts my feelings really badly because I try hard to like her. It has even made me cry. It seems like the only things she can say are stuff like how horrible we are and how we talk too much. We either ask too many questions or not enough. Worst of all, she talks about how wonderful her other class is. I can't tell her how I feel because I would never be able to look at her again."

Age 11

Dr. Deak: If this girl's account is accurate, she has a legitimate issue. It can be very difficult for a girl to deal with an adult who is causing conflict, especially an adult with a good deal of power and authority, such as a teacher or a sports coach.

If your daughter is in this kind of environment at school or on a sports team, help her find a way to communicate with the adult about the unintended effect the adult's behavior is having. You might help your daughter draft a note to the

eg: 106 What I Wish You Knew

teacher or coach explaining her feelings. There should be an advisor or trusted adult at school to whom she can talk to get added insight about how to proceed. Your daughter might allow you to talk personally with the teacher or coach. After all this thinking and talking with your daughter, you might find out that was all she wanted from you!

"I'm angry about being ignored."
"I am shy in class, so it takes a lot of effort to raise my hand and ask a question. When I am ignored, I get angry and feel like giving up."
Age 14

Dr. Deak: If this girl was eight years old, I would advise her parents to strategize with the teacher about how and when to call on her to increase her confidence and ability to speak out. A teacher working behind the scenes could pair her in projects with kids who will relate to her, or give her minor parts in plays to draw her out. But by eighth or ninth grade, it is important that parents get involved *directly* in school matters only when it is crucial. By this time, if a child has a social or personality issue, it is most likely centered on the individual, not the school. At age 14, it is better to help a girl figure out how to overcome shyness enough to be more forceful or to be noticed in a group.

Teach your daughter about the positive effects of body language, how and where she sits in class, and how to make eye contact. Practice with her. Consider getting her involved in a performance-based activity such as music, public speaking, or martial arts.

Encourage her to ask the teacher if she can have a few minutes before or after class or at lunch to ask a few questions. This will help her feel caught up. To improve her chances of being called on, consider this technique I have used: Make a seating chart of the class, and have her spend a couple of days tracking who the teacher calls on, where they sit, and why it seems those kids were chosen. Look at the teacher's patterns together, and talk about what your daughter can do to improve her chances of getting called on. As she comes home with new data each day, it becomes a fun problem to solve and strategize together.

"Kids treat me badly because I'm smart."

"I go to a gifted program once a week, and I try hard to keep straight As. The problem is people think I'm a goody two-shoes because I always do my work. I am confused because I think I should want to do well. I don't know how to respond to them."

Age 11

Dr. Deak: To an 11-year-old who is thinking in black-and-white terms about what is right and wrong, this situation just does not make sense. Doing well should be right and be reinforced as a good thing. But now many of her peers are saying it is bad. It is important to explain that some people hide insecurity or jealousy by making fun of someone who is smart and productive. That may not be as fulfilling an answer as your daughter would like, but it will get tucked away in her cortex and over time can have a positive effect on her.

Help her formulate some responses to teasing. The comments usually stop if she can give a response that is clear and has some force or humor. Start with something lighthearted and work with her until she finds a response she feels comfortable saying. I always tell girls that if they have an answer, no one will make more than three comments or tease them more than three times before it stops. I have not been wrong yet!

"I'm no good at this."

"I am really bad at math, and I have to get a tutor and go to summer school. I don't like not being smart, and I don't know what to do."

Age 11

Dr. Deak: Math—and much of learning—is like a jigsaw puzzle: you often can't see the picture clearly until you put together enough of the pieces. This girl needs to know that just because she struggles in one subject doesn't mean she should label herself unintelligent. She is working to put together more of the puzzle pieces by getting additional help; that is a sign of strength and willingness to learn, not of weakness.

For many girls, wanting to perfect things or understand them right away interferes with learning or sticking with the subject. This applies in both academics and athletics. Empathize with your

daughter's feelings of embarrassment, and then communicate that
learning something, or improving
at it, requires making mistakes,
trying again, and not really knowing the answer at first. Point out
that even the smartest or most
athletic girls have other skills they
wish they could improve.

If your daughter struggles with
math in particular, it does not
mean she will never succeed in
the subject. Several years ago,
female math specialists were
interviewed, and most said that
math was hard for them in middle
school, high school, or both. They
spoke of having to work hard, and
some even had tutors. Eventually
it clicked with them, and they
developed not only an understanding but a passion for the subject.
Your daughter may not develop a
full-blown love affair with the subject or sport she struggles in, but
let her know that the clouds can
indeed part if she continues to
work toward understanding.

**"My learning disability makes
me feel bad."**
*"I have attention deficit disorder
and lots of kids at my school know.
Sometimes they treat me like I'm
a dweeb and it makes me upset.*

*A lot of the time I feel confused and
irritated at people."*
Age 11
**Dr. Deak: Attention deficit
disorder (ADD) or attention deficit
hyperactivity disorder (ADHD)**
used to be considered more of an
issue for boys, but now we know
it affects just as many girls.
Because girls with ADD may
appear passive, quiet, or not interested in participating, they are
often not diagnosed until they hit
the academic wall. It is important
to recognize that if a child has
an attention disorder, it is not an
issue of intelligence or ability but
one of organization of thoughts
and being able to keep the brain
tuned in to the task at hand. If
you determine your daughter has
ADD, have her evaluated by medical and educational specialists.
Medication can be very helpful in
getting the part of the brain that
is the "tuner" to work more effectively. The end result is clearer
thinking, better productivity, and
less irritability. One girl described
it to me as "putting glasses on
your brain."

If your daughter has ADD,
an education specialist can help
you find techniques to improve her
classroom performance. It may

help if she sits in an area with fewer distractions, gets written rather than oral instructions from her teacher, or gets extra time on tests. If she has ADHD, finding activities in which she can release excess energy can help her hyperactivity. With help, ADD children can learn to monitor their attention and become focused when their attention wanders.

The sad reality is that ADD and ADHD are often misunderstood by adults and especially by peers. Give your daughter language to explain her condition. She might try, "My mind organizes things differently than most people's." Or "Sometimes ADD makes it hard for me to stay focused on the work at hand."

It is also helpful if you—or the teacher—talk about ADD or ADHD in relation to differing learning styles. One parent group I know paid for a workshop for teachers and a special presentation about how the brain works for students. Students analyzed their learning styles and figured out what study techniques worked best for them. This helped kids understand that some brains work differently.

"I have too much to do."

"I am so busy! I have to fit piano, drama practice, reading, swimming, and homework into my schedule. I never get around to doing everything I need to do. Sometimes I don't even have time to sit down and think."
Age 11

Dr. Deak: Having time to think and reflect is just as important as all of the enriching activities available for our children. In fact, many psychologists make the case that an overprogrammed existence can be very detrimental for children. By the time middle school starts and the homework level increases, the number of choices your daughter is making from the smorgasbord of activities should decrease. Selecting only one or two activities during the school year is an important decision-making and prioritizing skill to learn. Try the "Rule of Three": no more than three evenings of structured activities each week.

Schools are even questioning the quantity of homework given to students. Some schools are experimenting with no homework at all or none on weekends to allow more time for family, reading, and playing. So far, the research is quite positive about the beneficial effects of this policy on children and their families. And, surprisingly, reducing homework does not seem to reduce learning or achievement on standardized tests.[2]

"My parents put a lot of pressure on me."

"I'm on the track team, and my parents give me a lot of constructive criticism. They tell me to change everything about how I run. "Keep your arms down, feet straight! Breathe through your nose! Get a longer stride!" Sometimes it makes me feel like I'm an awful runner, when deep inside I know I'm good at it."

Age 14

Dr. Deak: The love we have for our daughters is incredibly intense. We care so much! That may be why this girl's mother and father got carried away and tried to be running coaches instead of parents. In the booklet "A Parent's Guide to Girls' Sports," put out by the Women's Sports Foundation, female professional athletes talk about how much their parents contributed to their success: by having confidence in them, consoling them when they faltered, encouraging them to continue trying, driving to lessons and games, and sitting through rain and snow to watch them play. When you read their words, you know how important parents are to their kids' achievement in the short and long run. Unless she specifically asks for your help, once your daughter is past the ball-tossing stage of early childhood, giving her skill development advice is usually ineffective and often counterproductive. Leave that to her coach.

The same lesson applies to your daughter's experience in the classroom. She needs your support and confidence more than daily reminders on how to improve her physics grade.

"I'm really competitive."

"I really like to win, especially in sports like volleyball, softball, and swimming. I find lots of things naturally easy to do, but I'm also

2. Etta Kralovec and John Buell, *The End of Homework: How Homework Disrupts Families, Overburdens Children, and Limits Learning* (Boston: Beacon Press, August 2000).

very hard on myself. When I make a mistake, I don't stop to realize that everyone makes errors, even people who are in the spotlight. I put a lot of pressure on myself."
Age 13

Dr. Deak: For a girl who has decent athletic talent, this kind of budding perfectionism can sometimes interfere with performance. When athletically talented girls are young, they excel in sports compared to most of their peers. By middle school, many girls who feel they do not have natural athletic talent drop out of the sports scene. The boys who used to be physically and developmentally smaller than girls their age now have caught up and can provide stiff competition. So, for a girl who cares about excelling in sports, the odds have changed. She is probably participating mostly with other equally talented girls and boys. Now, for the first time, an athletically talented girl may begin to meet obstacles, make some mistakes, lose, and not be able to count on her talent alone to put her in the winner's circle.

Parents, get out your "fine line" walking shoes. Your daughter needs you to take her seriously.

You can start by asking "What can I do to help?" to let her know you understand, care, and are willing to do whatever you can. Consider providing individual lessons and working with a professional in a particular sport. If you choose your pro well, she or he will help your daughter accept losing and making mistakes, as well as helping her strive to improve.

"Competing is hard for me."
"I think it is ridiculous to try to compete, because someone will always be better than you."
Age 14

Dr. Deak: Not everyone is driven to win, and thank goodness for that—we would not want a world composed *entirely* of competitive types. On the other hand, doing as well as one can is very much related to the working world and to having a healthy and happy life. The parents of a noncompetitive girl need to accept their daughter's core makeup but also help her find something she is so interested in that she will work hard for it. That will help her give her best and stretch her abilities. For this type of girl, trying to use competition or winning as a motivational tool is a no-win proposition for parents and pure frustration for their daughter.

But if the statement made by the girl who wrote this letter is defense for feeling incompetent or fearful of competition, her parents' approach should be quite different. There are two effective strategies that you can try if your daughter feels this way, and they are similar to techniques used for dealing with phobias. (After all, this is just a mild version of fear of failure.) "Flooding" is like jumping in the deep water. "Desensitization" is wading in. An example of flooding would be to have your daughter sign up for an Outward Bound trip. Through outdoor adventure experiences, she would have to face striving, risking, and fear. Outward Bound has many examples of girls coming back much more courageous and able to handle competition and risk-taking.

Wading in is what teachers and parents do all during the child-rearing years. You encourage, cajole, and inspire her to take lessons and try things that are difficult and new. If you can get her to try, and then she experiences some success, she will continue to get stronger.

"Are boys better than girls at sports?"

"In gym class, the teacher often discriminates against girls. She says things like, "We can't play girls versus boys because we all know who's going to win." It makes me feel bad that there are people who still think boys are better athletes than girls. I am one of the best basketball players out of the girls, and I could beat most or all of the boys."
Age 13

Dr. Deak: This teacher's statement definitely reinforces negative stereotypes. Of course you want your daughter to respect her teachers, but this is one occasion when you may want to suggest that her teacher's ideas are out of date. If she is a quiet kid, she may choose to rebut the teacher's comment in her head. If she is outspoken, coach her about disagreeing politely. She might say something like, "You know, some girls play pretty good basketball. Look at Sheryl Swoopes." If she feels comfortable talking to the teacher, she may want to let him or her know how those sexist comments make her feel.

At home, you can talk about different kinds of strength—for

example, about endurance (which most girls have) versus muscle mass (which most boys have). You can discuss upper-body strength (which most boys develop at this age) and lower-body strength (which most girls have and which can make them powerful runners or rock climbers). Be sure to point out strong, outstanding female athletes on television, at sporting events, and in magazines such as *Sports Illustrated for Women*.

Humor also goes a long way. If your daughter tells you about derogatory comments she has heard about women's strength, point out an exceptionally strong or strong-willed woman in your family. You might say, "That's right, all girls are wimps, and your Grandmother Jean is a wilting daisy!" Making light of demeaning ideas allows you to dismiss them and to create a bond between the two of you.

YOUR ROLE

Form a partnership with her school. Don't wait for a problem to arise. Schedule an appointment early in the year to talk about your daughter's goals, to express your hopes, and to get advice from the teacher.

Help your daughter find her "person." I encourage every girl I meet to have an adult to whom she can talk about school issues, one she respects and who she feels cares about her. It can be the nurse, a secretary, or her gym teacher—someone who is on the spot and has special insight into the personalities and workings of the classrooms.

Help her find her "North Star." Mary Pipher, author of *Reviving Ophelia,* uses this term to refer to a girl's passion, be it horseback riding or designing gardens. A passion will help her stay healthy when the bumps of life come along. When her friend deserts her, going to the barn and having her horse nuzzle her makes the day livable. The catch: you cannot choose your daughter's North Star.

Don't overschedule her. No one argues about the positive effects that enriching activities have on girls' lives. But check in regularly with yourself and your daughter about how much is enough.

Understand learning styles. What works for you may not work for your daughter. Get a learning styles inventory test from her school, and take it together. Once you understand how both of you think, you will be better able to help her with homework and organization.

Help her get physical. More than anything else, doing something in a performance mode makes a girl stronger. It could be a sport, but it can also be a camping trip or dance lesson. The choice of

activity almost doesn't matter—doing is the key. Encourage
your daughter to do at least one thing each school year and
each summer.

Listen carefully. When your daughter is facing a struggle in the
classroom or on the playing field, the dilemma is whether to listen,
help, or fix it. Start with listening and keep going gently and carefully, feeling your way until you both are satisfied. The more you
fix, the less she learns.

CHAPTER

Dealing with Difficult Times
by Roni Cohen-Sandler, Ph.D.

> *"I worry so much about the future. What's going to happen?*
> *Will the world end soon? Will my house burn down?*
> *Will sixth grade be cool, freaky, or scary? It stresses me out."*
> Age 10

Coping with distressing life events, whether real or imagined, current or anticipated, can be especially hard for our adolescent daughters. As girls adjust to dramatic changes in their own bodies, emotional lives, schools, and friendships, they usually crave predictability and security in their environment. The last thing they need is more stress. That is one reason your daughter may react to difficult situations and losses as if her very world is caving in around her.

No matter how you try to protect your daughter, she will inevitably experience uncertainty, hardship, and even heartache. As she becomes more mature, she will understand both the exciting and tragic possibilities in her life, but along with this awareness comes vulnerability. As she begins to reflect and think abstractly, her problems can seem magnified. Learning to master stressful experiences will definitely spur her social and emotional growth, but when she faces tough situations for the first time, she may become anxious, self-doubting, and helpless when she most wants to feel in control.

The girl whose letter opens this chapter poignantly expresses a multitude of fears about the life ahead of her. Like many girls her age, she finds it scary to think about what her future might hold and what novel or devastating situations she may encounter. Overwhelmed, she visits one possible catastrophe after another. How can she manage if she doesn't know what will happen? Poised on the precipice of early adolescence, she uses the powerful image of her home burning down to symbolize a common fear: the sudden loss of basic childhood security.

This young girl is clearly worried about being safe as she grows up. If she keeps her disturbing thoughts to herself, though, she will probably feel isolated, abnormal, and thus more afraid. She may feel better just by voicing her fears. If your daughter is feeling similar distress, comfort her by listening with empathy and taking her concerns seriously. As she becomes less anxious, she will feel more prepared to tackle the circumstances that come her way.

Dealing with Stress

Besides trying to keep up with her studies, obey her parents, and get along with her siblings, your daughter has two main missions: to learn what makes her unique and, at the same time, to fit in with her peers. As she explores her interests and discovers where she shines, she is also questioning how her achievements will affect her relationships. Will her friends and classmates admire her, or will she be teased if she is too accomplished? Can she become her own person and still make you proud? These sometimes contradictory demands can be stressful and confusing.

Adding fuel to the fire, many girls feel pressure to be super-stars in their own world. Your daughter may feel compelled to excel in every possible way: academically, socially, athletically, musically, artistically, and more. Her calendar may rival that of a harried CEO. On a daily basis, she must figure out where to channel her limited energy. Will practicing her free throw or violin pay off, or should she use that time to try for straight A's? As a busy parent, you know it's difficult, but show her how to strike a healthy balance between school, sports, hobbies, and socializing. Make sure she has downtime to reflect on new ideas, puzzle over changes, let off steam, and dream. Let her know you genuinely value her efforts by saying things like, "What's important is that you figure out what really satisfies you and makes you feel good about yourself. I don't expect you to be great at everything." She will relax when she sees that you appreciate her unique strengths.

> *"I am probably one of the most stressed-out kids around. After I go to my regular school, I go to a special Chinese school for extra classes. I have hours of homework, music lessons, clubs, and sports. Sometimes I am so overwhelmed I just want to scream! There is never a moment when I sit down and do nothing or don't worry."*
> Age 12

When they are preteens, the need to excel causes many girls to quit hobbies or sports they used to enjoy. "Since I'll never be a ballerina," my own daughter declared back then, flinging her toe shoes to the back of her closet, "why should I bother?" Give your daughter the freedom to simply enjoy herself rather than to be always working toward a goal. Nurture her love of adventure and her courage to try new paths. At the same time, remember that with the all-or-nothing thinking of adolescence, your daughter may act as if typical bumps in the road—a bad grade, strained friendship, or lost game—are utterly disastrous. Understand that

to her, small failures may represent dashed dreams. Help her to
see each disappointment or failure as only a temporary setback
along the vast road of opportunities ahead.

Violence in Her World

Since your daughter spends about seven hours per day in school,
you want her to feel comfortable and confident there. Yet, in light
of recent school violence, many teenagers think it is risky even to
board their school buses. The media's reports would have us
believe that students are routinely wielding deadly weapons on
playgrounds. The perception that schools are dangerous is perpet-
uated when uniformed guards are placed in hallways. While it is
true that more automatic weapons have been used in school shootings in recent years, your daughter may be relieved to learn that
the overall rate of school crime has actually decreased.[1]

To help her feel safer in school, speak with the school adminis-
trators about the precautions they are taking to reduce risks. One
middle schooler I know told her mother, "Nobody could do anything bad in our school because the teachers all stand in the halls
watching us." After you are assured of the staff's awareness and
responsiveness to dangers, you can truthfully tell your daughter,
"I can't guarantee nothing bad will ever happen, but your school is
doing everything possible to keep students safe." You might also
look into Warning Signs, the youth antiviolence community education program developed jointly by the American Psychological
Association and cable television's MTV.

While sensational violence does concern teenage girls, they
are actually more worried about more subtle, daily forms of

1. Joe Volz, "Media Distorts the Truth about Violence in School," *The American
Psychological Association Monitor* (October 1999): 21.

aggression such as teasing, bullying, and harassment. One study found that 89 percent of girls ages 9 to 19 were targets of suggestive jokes, comments, gestures, or looks.[2] Though no teenager is immune, girls who are deemed "different" are particularly at risk. You may recognize the signs of cruelty. But when the victim is your own daughter, her acute pain may be so difficult for you to hear that you want to gloss over it. Or your daughter may be too embarrassed to report ongoing bullying. Try extra hard not to lecture or blame her for what she is experiencing. Teach her that meanness is never acceptable. "You're terrific, and you have the right to be treated with respect," you might say.

> "At my school, people get in fights in the halls about once a month. A while back, this girl rode my bus home and tried to beat me up. She didn't end up hitting me, but she stood there and screamed at me. My school's dangerous, but I don't think any of us really know how dangerous."
>
> age 13

When your daughter was younger, you probably gave her lessons in emotional education. You showed her how to express anger properly—to talk it out rather than duke it out with her sister, for example. When she didn't share toys or tormented her little brother, you explained how her behavior affected others. Now that she is older, your role is to guide her to defuse others' hostility, to speak up for herself, and to ask for help when she needs it. Let her know you'll step in with school authorities or professional help, if necessary, to ensure her safety.

2. Nan Stein, Nancy L. Marshall, and Linda R. Tropp, *Secrets in Public: Sexual Harassment in Our Schools,* A Report on the Results of a *Seventeen* Magazine Survey, a joint project of NOW Legal Defense and Education Fund and Center for Research on Women, Wellesley College (March 1993).

Dealing with Hopelessness

We all want our daughters to be content and emotionally okay. That's why it is heartbreaking to hear your smart, capable daughter say, "I'm no good. I can't do anything right!" Or when she insists, despite her sweet nature, "Nobody likes me. I'm such a loser!" Your sincerest offers to help may be met with, "What's the use?"

What can make your daughter so sad, lonely, and hopeless? If your daughter struggles with difficult situations for which she is ill prepared, she may lose self-confidence. In many cases, depression results from severe or accumulated losses. Rifts in teenage friendships, betrayals, and rejections can leave gaping holes in her emotional armor. And because she wants to please you, she may fear that her "failures" will let you down and she will lose your love.

"I don't know what happened. I used to have good friends, and now we hardly speak to each other. I cry myself to sleep every night. When I go to the few birthday parties I am invited to, I never fit in. I just watch all the best friends and think, 'There was once a time when I was happy like them.' If only you knew how lonely and depressing it feels to be me."
Age 12

Biological factors may predispose some girls to the effects of stressful events. Depression can make your daughter feel overwhelmingly isolated and undermine her belief in her ability to make a difference in the world. Moreover, she may believe there is no hope of improvement. But because many girls hide such despair beneath a cheerful facade, recognizing the signs and getting your daughter appropriate help may be challenging. You, too, may wonder if what you are seeing is the normal moodiness of adolescence or genuine depression.

In general, the more striking the changes are in your daughter's attitude, the greater is your need to assess her further.

If you ask her directly, "Are you depressed?" don't be surprised if she not only says no but also takes offense. She may not identify with the word "depression" because she cannot relate to the exaggerated, near-comatose depressed inpatients portrayed in movies. Plus, she may not understand that her irritability, excessive guilt, plummeting grades, or pessimism are symptoms of depression. It can be better to observe, "You've seemed pretty down in the dumps lately. Are you feeling discouraged?" Other research shows that clinically depressed children often recognize their illness before their parents do. If your daughter is truly depressed, she may welcome your questions and be relieved that you have noticed the seriousness of her emotions.

The classic signs of depression include changes in appetite or sleep patterns. But you should also be alert for signs such as indecisiveness, apathy, and self-deprecation. Your daughter may demonstrate black-and-white thinking—logic that leads her to conclude, "If I am not perfect, I must be a failure." She may be weepy, moody, annoyed, or bored. She may withdraw from family members or friends, or lose interest in activities that used to give her pleasure. If in doubt about your daughter's emotional health, get professional help. Depression is a highly treatable problem.

Teetering on the Edge

As scary as depression is, the possibility of our daughters harming or killing themselves is nearly inconceivable to us. About half of teenagers polled say they have thought of suicide, and 20 percent have considered it seriously. Although adolescent males die more often by their own hands, females are four times as likely to make attempts. About 90 percent of girls who attempt suicide do so by taking pills, and most teenagers engage in self-destructive behavior in their own homes between 3 P.M. and 6 P.M.

Your daughter may be more susceptible to suicidal thoughts if she has been through prolonged family problems, suffered severe stress, or experienced intense conflicts that are out of her control. A recent study showed that extreme stress keeps children from developing effective problem-solving skills, which in turn causes the hopelessness that can predispose a young person to suicidal thinking. Suffering significant losses—or anticipating them—also places her at greater risk, as do depression, substance use, or acting aggressively. The most alarming signs of suicidal thinking are making preparations, giving away prized possessions, and saying good-byes.

Girls who hurt themselves are not "crazy." They are merely trying to cope with overwhelming stress. They may have tried to deal with their problems and failed, and they can't figure out what else to do. Thinking *Nothing else will help,* girls turn to suicide when they simply cannot tolerate further pain. Most often, they hope not to die but to make last-ditch efforts to communicate with important people in their lives. After conflicts with friends, boyfriends, or family members, a suicidal act essentially says, "I really need you to change your attitude or treat me differently, and I don't know how else to reach you." That's why it is so crucial to respond promptly to any worrisome behavior.

If you think your daughter might be considering suicide, be direct and open with her: "Are you thinking of hurting yourself?" It is a myth that mentioning suicide will put the idea in her head. In fact, showing her you are willing to talk about her pain is like throwing her a lifeline.

The good news is that you can give your daughter the support and comfort that are key to building trust and to protecting her from the harmful effects of stress. When she reacts to stress, accept her feelings nonjudgmentally, even if you don't agree with them. Reassure her that you love her, no matter what. Offer hope that you will help her find other ways to deal with her problems, using words such as, "Taking your own life would be a devastating, permanent answer to a very temporary situation. We can solve this together." Take any suicidal plans or behaviors seriously, and seek further evaluation. Contact the National Suicide Hotline (1-888-SUICIDE) or consult your local telephone book for suicide prevention and crisis intervention centers.

Coping with Losses

As your daughter grows and makes transitions in her development, she may feel loss at every step along the way. She may mourn the simplicity and security of childhood. As she meets girls who are prettier, smarter, faster, or more popular, she may lose an ideal vision of herself and, therefore, some self-esteem. With puberty, she even loses her once-familiar body. And what loss can seem greater than the one required for independence—when she will leave her parents and home behind?

Against this backdrop, the possibility of losing someone dear through death, divorce, or even moving away may feel to your daughter like more than she can bear. A potential loss can also intensify her growing sense of her own mortality. In fact, studies show that fearing or anticipating a loss is actually more stressful than the event itself. If your daughter loses a loved one—or fears that she will—she may become so emotionally drained by her efforts to cope that she has trouble concentrating, sleeping well, or performing up to par. This profound emotional experience can also set her apart from her peers, accentuating other differences and causing her to feel isolated.

With her blossoming thinking skills, your daughter may look for new and different ways to make sense of this loss. She may long to go beyond the explanations she previously accepted and delve into *why* loved ones might leave her.

If some of her questions catch you off guard, be honest about getting her a response. "I'm not sure about that," you may have to say, "but I promise to get some answers for you."

Because she is striving to be competent at everything she does, your daughter may also scrutinize her reactions to the loss to determine whether they are "appropriate." Is she caring enough? What if she does all the "right" things but loses the person anyway? What does she risk if she hopes for the best but the worst happens?

As your daughter questions if she can survive a divorce, death of a family member, or other loss, her fears may not be all that different from yours. You can model the healing power of sharing by expressing your own painful feelings. Tell her how you coped with similar situations in the past. Meanwhile, guide her to devote extra time to those she loves, offering a comforting squeeze or a loving hug. That way, she'll look back without regrets. Maintain a sense of normalcy by showing her it is okay to enjoy other activities and to feel pleasure.

> *"About a year ago, my mother was diagnosed with colon cancer. She had surgery and chemotherapy. It was very hard on my dad and me, but as a family we helped her pull through. Her doctors recently found spots that they think might be more cancer. I don't think I have the strength to help her through this again."*
> Age 10

When a Loved One Dies

The death of a loved one creates a chasm in your daughter's world. Cumulatively, such losses can shake her belief that *any* connection can endure. By age 10, girls know that death is permanent and irreversible. Regardless, your daughter may expect the deceased to somehow reappear; even after Grandma dies, your daughter may unthinkingly reach for the phone to relate a triumph to her. This is a common initial response, and it lets your daughter delay the emotional impact of the loss. Later, however, painful thoughts and memories can make her feel overwhelmed, forgetful, and even crazy. Educate her that this is normal and that everyone grieves in her own way.

Perhaps she feels guilty about what she did or didn't do when the person who died was alive. She may be angry at the world, at God, at herself, even at the person who passed away and abandoned her. Because other people can be intolerant of anger in girls, your daughter may need your help in accepting and understanding her fury. She wants to be grown-up, but assure her that crying is not babyish and can be a great relief.

> *"Ever since my dad died last year, my family has been fighting, yelling, and feeling frustrated. It's really hard on me. My whole body wants to shut down and run away to see my dad."*
> Age 10

Another possibility is that your daughter appears to take the death in stride, but then dissolves into tears when she can't find her favorite bracelet or her friend forgets to call. Further disappointments and losses, no matter how trivial, may trigger powerful emotions. It is sheer torture to watch your daughter struggle with her pain. But even if you could shelter her completely, you would not want to lose these opportunities to teach her vital lessons about death, mourning, and giving and receiving comfort.

Your daughter may also be troubled by mundane matters such as what to do, say, and even wear at funerals. Many girls fear they will laugh, show disrespect, or somehow make fools of themselves at the services. Help your daughter participate in these rituals. Teach her the power of simply holding the hand of a bereaved person and saying, "I'm sorry for your loss." When she offers support by sending a condolence card or note, shopping for groceries for the deceased's family, or making a scrapbook about the person she lost, she copes actively with her own grief. Teach her that letting go of pain is not the same as letting go of the person who died. She will forever keep the deceased "alive" by nourishing her memories.

Through all these experiences, your daughter will learn to identify and manage her own reactions, empathize with others' feelings, and see adults as both good listeners and sources of emotional support. As she uses these vital skills to deal successfully with difficult times, she will feel more confident in her ability to handle the inevitable challenges in her life.

Dr. Roni Cohen-Sandler is the author of **"I'm Not Mad, I Just Hate You!"** *She is a mother and a clinical psychologist specializing in the issues of women and adolescent girls. She is also author of a forthcoming book on mothers, daughters, and teenage social lives.*

LISTENING IN

Dr. Cohen-Sandler explores how you can help your daughter cope with pressure-filled situations, depression, and fears of violence and death.

"I'm overwhelmed."

"I don't have to be the best, but if I'm not, then my parents won't like me as much. I know a lot of the pressure I feel comes from myself, because I feel really good when I know I'm on top and good at things. I feel I have to stay that way. Some pressure comes from my parents, because my sister's grades dropped in fifth grade, and now they don't think she's good at anything."

Age 11

Dr. Cohen-Sandler: During adolescence, our daughters face the tricky tasks of figuring out their own true talents and goals and, at the same time, sifting through the various messages they get from us, their loving but sometimes unwittingly unhelpful parents. We make mistakes because our job is equally difficult: helping our daughters be all that they can be while respecting their right to be themselves.

This girl questions what drives her to excel—the personal satisfaction she gets from her achievements or the hope that they will earn her more of her parents' love. Like most girls, she is influenced less by what her parents say than by her astute observations of how they act. Having reaped the rewards of success before, she feels even more compelled to maintain her excellence. Since she is actively trying to sort everything out, however, this girl is already ahead of the game.

It's natural to encourage and sometimes prod our daughters, but we must be careful not to convey the message "You are your achievements" or "My love is contingent on your success." That would be an unfair burden. Our love should be unconditional. Support your daughter as she defines her true passions and limitations. When you assure her she doesn't have to achieve to please you, you give her the freedom to explore her individuality. Chances are, this gift will allow her to blossom.

"My mom plays the piano and, boy, is she good at it. When I first

started to play, I wanted to be just like her. When I found out I wasn't as good as she was, I stressed myself out practicing things I couldn't play. I wanted her to be really proud of me. When I told my mom this, she said she was proud of me no matter how well I play the piano."

Age 11

Dr. Cohen-Sandler: As your daughter forms her identity, she may try to match your talents and successes. While our daughters' admiration can be quite flattering and gratifying to us as parents, what pressure it places on our girls! If you face a similar situation, help your daughter see that she is comparing her still-developing skills to an adult's mastery. No wonder your accomplishments seem effortless to her! Remind her that you, too, got discouraged, struggled, and even flopped on occasion. Perhaps your daughter needs further time before her talents equal yours. Or maybe, as our letter writer suggests, your specialty is not really her thing, but she is twisting herself in knots anyway to make you happy.

It's great that this girl could tell her mother how she felt, and even better that her mom could set her straight. Clarify to your daughter that you are proud of her for who she is, not just for what she does. Playing the piano, painting, or writing does not define her. You value her inner qualities—her honesty, spunk, compassion, and fun-loving spirit. It is tempting to live vicariously through our children. Though you may harbor secret hopes for your daughter, give her a different message: "Feel free to explore what you enjoy. I'll help you and even be the president of your fan club, but I don't need you to become something for me. I love you the way you are."

"I am stressed out because my cheerleading adviser wants me to learn flips and handsprings, but I can't even do them on the trampoline. So she signed me up for gymnastics camp, and I don't want to go. I even have to pay with my own money! She is putting too much pressure on me. I'm just not ready for it."

Age 13

Dr. Cohen-Sandler: We know that mentors can bless our daughters with many benefits. One of the most wonderful messages we can give girls is "There are fabulous women out there, besides me, who have much to teach you." And yet you must help your daughter evaluate whether her mentor's advice is right for her. Mentors can offer invaluable expertise, but girls are the ultimate experts on themselves. This girl clearly believes her adviser is neither listening to her nor attuned to her feelings. She feels pushed well beyond where she feels competent and comfortable. This is not a position we want to see our daughters in.

It is tough to know when to support a mentor's opinion and when to intervene. Try to assess whether your daughter needs a gentle push to overcome a hurdle in her training or needs to trust her gut about not being ready. You might ask, "Are you able to talk to your adviser about your feelings?" Coach her on what to say to feel more prepared. Ultimately you may need to step in to make sure that her desires are taken seriously and she doesn't lose interest or burn out in her sport.

"I'm scared."

"My dad is an alcoholic, and he doesn't know what he puts me through. Once some kids at school were pretending to be drunk in front of me. I wanted to tell them to shut up. I felt like curling up in a corner and crying. I want to pray for him aloud in church, but I don't want everyone to know he is an alcoholic. I don't know what to do."
Age 12

Dr. Cohen-Sandler: Many girls whose parents have serious problems suffer silently, keeping their pain to themselves out of loyalty to family. This girl acknowledges that her father's imperfections hurt her, yet she still feels protective of him. Unfortunately, the stigma of alcoholism puts this girl in a terrible quandary. Although she clearly needs help, her need to maintain a family secret prevents her from getting the comfort and support of friends. Instead, she feels humiliated as she imagines how her classmates view her. When girls feel judged and shamed by a parent's problem, they tend to withdraw from peers at a time when they most need to feel included. It is easy to see why this girl sounds so sad, helpless, and desperate.

If someone in your family is suffering from such an illness, your daughter is undoubtedly suffering, too. Although you may think that ignoring the problem will diminish it, the only way to ease your daughter's distress is to talk openly.

Find ways for your daughter to get the help she needs without divulging secrets. Give her permission to speak with trusted individuals. Enroll her in an adolescent support group offered by a mental health organization in your community. Alateen is one national organization offering help for young people who are relatives or friends of problem drinkers.

"Once a boy brought a gun to my school. He was caught before anybody was hurt, but it was scary. I still don't know why it happened, but I believe it's partly because most teachers and principals don't really pay attention to students and what they're involved in."
Age 14

Dr. Cohen-Sandler: During adolescence, our daughters' idealism and belief in their own immortality can be shattered by traumatic events. This girl is unsettled. Aside from inciting the obvious fears, the incident at her school has forced her to reevaluate what she can expect from adults in her life. Most teenagers are ambivalent about the amount of privacy and assistance they want from adults. Your daughter might say, "I don't need you or my teachers telling me what to do!" Yet she may be outraged when these "unnecessary" adults fail to protect her. Secretly, she may still wish for her parents to be all-knowing and all-powerful. Don't be shocked, therefore, if your daughter blames you for not preventing the bad things that happen in her life. She wishes you could protect her, but she hates the fact that she needs you!

Empathize with her fears. Try words like, "I know these are scary times. It's awful to think of someone becoming violent in your school. It can make it hard to trust people. But these terrible stories teach all of us to understand how angry and excluded some students feel, to be kinder, and to reach out before tragedies occur."

"I understand why things like school shootings happen. It's not the parents', teachers', or media's fault. It's the fault of kids. I know what it's like to go to school and get ridiculed, slammed into lockers, made fun of, and spit on just because of the clothes you wear, the classes you take, and whether or not you're an athlete. People are being treated like this every day. It's not going to stop, and certain kids are going to continue to say,

*'I'm not going to take this anymore,'
and end up taking their own life or
someone else's."*
Age 14

Dr. Cohen-Sandler: This girl knows
all too well how it feels to be the
victim of ongoing harassment
and abuse. She is outraged by
how students behave toward one
another. She also seems hopeless
about her ability to improve these
circumstances. Her words make
me think she can relate to the
seething rage that is often a pre-
cursor to aggression. She might
harbor fantasies of retaliation
against those who mistreat her. In
fact, when she writes that "certain
kids are going to . . . end up taking
their own life," it strikes me that
she understands such desperation
because she has experienced it
firsthand. I worry that this girl may
try to hurt herself.

If your daughter confesses to
having such thoughts, assure her
they are normal. But differentiate
between having hostile or self-
harming thoughts and acting on
them. Don't hesitate to get a professional opinion as to the seriousness of these concerns. Confer
with your daughter's guidance
counselor or school psychologist
to help you understand what is

really going on. How is she inter-
acting with her classmates? Is she
at risk? She could join a counseling group to learn how to protect
herself better. Taking courses in
assertiveness, self-defense, or
martial arts can also help.

"I'm really struggling!"

*"I have good parents and a nice
room, and I go to a nice school. But
I get depressed a lot about friends,
family, school, my sister, and myself.
My sister says I'm a loner, and these
kids who used to be my friends now
call me an outcast. There's a group
of girls at school who are mean to
me. I have no confidence, so I don't
think I can do anything."*
Age unknown

Dr. Cohen-Sandler: On the surface,
this girl believes she has the
basics she needs to be happy. But
she articulates what many girls
feel at this age—the disparity
between the superficial appearance of her life and what she feels
inside. She is in significant pain
because she thinks she is a failure. At a time when one of a girl's
most important sources of esteem
is the quality of her relationships,
she seems isolated. It is hard to
know which came first: her lack of
confidence or her isolation from

peers. Either way, restoring her confidence and friendships can go hand in hand.

When your daughter goes through a rough patch, you may feel helpless to make things better for her, but you are not. Encourage her to have a classmate over or to invite someone she likes to the movies. Help her enroll in extracurricular activities that are not only enjoyable but may boost her confidence and may also introduce her to other girls her age. Many girls find solace in volunteering to help less fortunate people. Professional therapy is another viable option.

"Now that I'm growing up, I've started to notice my feelings hurt a lot more. My parents are divorced, and when they broke up, I cried myself to sleep. I miss my dad very much, and it's hard to get over it. My grades are going down. My grandmother was diagnosed with colon cancer, and I don't want to lose her. I feel alone. I lock myself in my room and cry for hours. I'm tired of crying for my dad. I need help."
Age 12

Dr. Cohen-Sandler: This girl is understandably overwhelmed by the many losses she is experiencing. Her distress is to be expected; these are serious problems even for an adult to manage. It is not surprising that she does not have the wherewithal she once had to concentrate on her studies; grief itself is really hard work. But it is tragic that this girl feels alone. Single parents, trying to cope with such crises by themselves, can be so consumed that they miss signs that their daughters are in trouble. Don't put your relationship with your daughter on a back burner. Stay closely connected so that you know what she is doing when she locks herself in her room "for hours." It is okay not to know what to say or do. Try, "I'm so sorry to see you so sad. Do you want to talk about it?" or "What can I do to help?"

Also, it is important to recognize that earlier losses can make your daughter more sensitive to later losses. Each loss successively re-evokes earlier pain, thereby intensifying grief. If your daughter is still suffering six months to a year after a loss, she may need professional help.

"I've lost almost all hope."
"I've been through a lot in my life. I don't know my birth father, I've been sexually harassed in school,

*and my stepdad (who drinks)
told me I was a disappointment to
the whole family. I don't eat sometimes, and once I thought it would
be better if I was dead, so I cut
myself on purpose. It would make
me happy if I had someone to talk
to or comfort me."*
Age 12

Dr. Cohen-Sandler: Sadly, this girl
has had multiple negative relationships with men. She aches for a
father she doesn't know and is
demeaned by an alcoholic step-
father. Along with the fact that
she has been sexually harassed,
her history makes me think she
does not believe she deserves to
be treated well. She also has not
been guided in how to protect
herself. If positive changes cannot
be made within the family, even
with family therapy, she should
be encouraged to build a healthy
relationship with a favorite uncle,
grandfather, or friend's father.

More urgently, this girl's
mother needs to recognize that
her daughter's isolation and sense
of helplessness are leading to
thoughts of killing herself. In
desperation, this girl has deprived
herself of food and cut herself.
Although these acts were not fatal,
they were pleas for help that seem

to have gone unanswered. Unless
she gets help soon, she could
progress to more lethal suicidal
behavior. If her mom is unable to
provide the help she needs, perhaps a loving relative or school
counselor could step in.

*"Earlier this year, death practically
consumed my every thought. I hated
the world. I hated myself. I hated
the people around me. Every little
thing ticked me off. I didn't care
about anything anymore. I hardly
ever spoke, and if I did I said something mean and hateful. I wrote a
lot, just pouring myself onto paper.
At home, I went on the Internet
and talked to people just like me
and wrote depressing poetry. But
now I've really seen both sides of
the story. I know now that there is
light at the end of the tunnel."*
Age 13

Dr. Cohen-Sandler: More than
adults, adolescents may display
depression through their irritability, anger, and hatefulness.
This girl describes other common
symptoms, such as being with-
drawn and apathetic. But despite
her pain, she took positive steps
that ultimately helped her. Her
writing became a safe outlet for
hostile thoughts and feelings that

would have been destructive to share aloud. Writing clarified her emotions, giving them reassuring shape and order. She even channeled her pain into creative efforts such as poetry.

Her other constructive approach was to commiserate with others who understood her distress. Her ability to connect saved her from further isolation and despair. If your daughter experiences similar problems, encourage her to join a support group, where she will get empathy and validation from others who have been in her shoes. Most of the time, depression lifts within six months. As this girl expresses, when the darkness recedes there is a greater appreciation for the depth of others' sadness, as well as renewed optimism and hopefulness.

"I may lose a person I love."
"My stepdad has had cancer for two years, but now he is at the end. He is very grumpy and tired. I have talked to my mom, my real dad, and my friends, and I've cried a lot. My friends give me all the support they can, but they don't know what it's like. It's so sad seeing him die, and I can't do anything about it.

I don't know what my life will be like without him. I feel like I'm not doing anything! I want to be there when he dies, and my mom says I can do that, but I don't know how it will affect me. I don't know what to do."
Age 11

Dr. Cohen-Sandler: Watching a loved one die is tragic, but this girl is getting through the ordeal as well as possible. Although she feels helpless to make the situation better and uneasy about how she will react in the future, her family is helping her use many good coping strategies. She feels comfortable turning to her friends and family. Even though she gets support from them, she is realistic about the fact that they cannot empathize perfectly when they haven't been through this experience. And that's okay with her.

If your daughter is losing someone important, allow her as much exposure to the situation as she feels comfortable with. Because of our own anxiety about death and dying, we tend to shield our daughters from such "unpleasantness." However, this tactic communicates that there is something to be afraid of rather than that death is a normal part of the life cycle.

If she wishes, give your daughter the chance to help a family member to die with dignity, surrounded by loved ones.

"My mom has cancer. It has made her so bigheaded that she forgets about me. I know it's hard for her to deal with it, but I want to be treated like her daughter again."
Age unknown

Dr. Cohen-Sandler: When someone is seriously ill, there are often enormous changes in the family's dynamics. Between pressing medical issues, treatment, and prolonged recuperation, it is easy to overlook needs that seem minor or even trivial. This can be especially true of emotional needs.

This girl is expressing feelings that are perfectly normal to have when a primary caretaker is sick. Although she doesn't express sadness and worry, it doesn't mean she doesn't feel them. It is important not to interpret her feelings as immature or selfish. It is natural for her to be anxious when her security is threatened. When an ailing parent is attending to the task of getting well, her concentration and energy are siphoned from her children. So instead of being able to rely on Mom for mundane needs like a ride to the mall or new jeans, not to mention for nurturing and advice, this girl has to do more for herself. In fact, if illness has reversed the mother-daughter roles, she may feel responsible for her mother's well-being. If your daughter seems irritated or impatient in this kind of situation, understand that her world changed dramatically without her say-so. She just wants life to return to normal.

"I'm dealing with a horrible loss."
"Ever since my mom died seven months ago, I have been so sad. I don't know what to do. I'm getting bad grades, I'm bad at soccer and basketball, and at my last dentist appointment, I had five cavities. I am bad at everything. I haven't told my dad how I feel, but I have told my nanny. I feel like the saddest person in my whole town."
Age 10

Dr. Cohen-Sandler: For a little girl, losing a mother is like having her worst nightmare come true. This girl's grief is palpable and colors her whole world. Her pain is so acute that she cannot imagine it lessening over time. If your daughter is intensely affected by a death, assure her that her grief will not last forever: "I know how much it hurts now. It feels like it'll never be different. But you are a strong girl, and you'll adjust. Maybe it won't happen for a while, but someday it'll hurt a lot less than it does now." You also may want to prepare her for grief's uneven course. She may feel a surge of renewed pain on birthdays, anniversaries, holidays, and other special occasions, especially during the first year.

Like this bereaved girl, your daughter may hesitate to share her pain with other survivors. She may fear making their grief worse or feel guilty about adding to their problems. You can tell her, "When someone dies, loved ones need each other more than ever. When we comfort each other, we also comfort ourselves."

"When my best friend died, I was so distraught. I felt like, 'Why wasn't it me?' But I got stronger. I wrote poems and did small things in remembrance of my friend. This made me feel better about the situation."
Age 14

Dr. Cohen-Sandler: Losing a best friend for any reason is stressful for a teenager, but a death is par-

ticularly devastating. The closer our daughters are in age or situation to the deceased, the more they can relate to the person who died and, therefore, the more shattering the death can be. If your daughter identifies with the deceased, she can develop survivor guilt. This girl, for example, felt guilty simply because she was still living while her best friend suffered and died.

Fortunately, this girl has worked through her grief productively. If your daughter loses someone important, she, too, may find it healing to write about what the deceased meant to her, the void the person left in her life, and what she wants to remember most. You also might suggest that she find small ways to honor and remember her friend.

YOUR ROLE

Use your reactions. Don't suppress the emotional responses you have to your daughter's problem. Use them as clues to what she's experiencing. If you feel overwhelmed, scared, or discouraged by her story, she probably feels that way, too.

Invite emotion. Emphasize to your daughter that while pain and grief are difficult to bear, they are never fatal. Denying or burying feelings, though, can cause them to fester and cause harmful physical symptoms.

Keep your fear in check. It's natural to feel fear when your daughter faces difficult times. That may make you yell, minimize problems, or cut off discussions. Recognize and contain your own apprehension before you talk with your daughter.

Avoid quick fixes. Your daughter needs to feel capable, so try not to step in quickly and fix her problems. Don't offer advice unless she asks for it. Instead, try, "Would you like to hear my thoughts?"

Encourage creativity. Give your daughter outlets for expressing her feelings, such as a journal or art materials. Parents tend to feel uncomfortable about dark poetry and gloomy music, but they may help your daughter work through her sadness or fears.

Discourage rescuing. When your daughter cares deeply about friends and wants to be seen as capable, she may try to take on others' problems. Raised to be nurturing, she may want to do good deeds and even save people. But when others' problems are too big, she can feel guilty and get discouraged.

Use all available help. Seek advice from anyone with expertise or personal experience. Get books and resources that explain difficult issues at an age-appropriate level for your daughter. Or find helpful sites on the Internet together.

Be good to yourself. In crises, it is easy to become deluged by responsibilities. Show your daughter that it is acceptable and desirable to take care of yourself. Be her role model by taking a walk or enjoying a book or bath to combat stress.

Rethink values. The silver lining of difficult times is that they force us to rethink what is most important to us. Talk with your daughter about calling an estranged friend, accepting help from relatives, or renewing comforting spiritual or religious connections.

Taking Risks: Cigarettes, Drugs, and Alcohol

by Lynn Ponton, M.D.

> *"I drank alcohol before and liked it, but I knew it was wrong.*
> *I felt like I was cheating everyone when I drank, so I promised*
> *myself I wouldn't do it again. But at my older friend's birthday*
> *party, she encouraged me to drink until, finally, I felt that I would*
> *be unpopular if I didn't. I did it to please her, but I regret it.*
> *I think kids turn to harmful substances so early because they*
> *are made to look cool by the media and advertising,*
> *so young people want them."*
>
> *Age 13*

Using alcohol, tobacco, or other drugs is a form of risk taking. Understanding why and how girls take risks has been the subject of my work as a psychiatrist for more than 20 years. It has also been an important area in my personal life, as I parent two teenage daughters. Both boys and girls take various risks as a way of developing and defining themselves. They take on new challenges in areas they understand little about and engage in behaviors with consequences ranging from devastating to extremely positive. This vital process begins in childhood but culminates during the adolescent years. Taking risks helps your daughter become independent from you and separate from her childhood, and it affects all aspects of her development—physical, psychological, social, sexual, and cultural.

The girl struggling in our opening letter helps us see the conflict many girls feel. She knows drinking is dangerous, yet to some degree she enjoys it because of the increased status she gains. It is not unusual that she feels pressured by friends to drink. Many girls first drink, smoke, or use drugs in a social setting with friends close by, watching. Your daughter may face a similar struggle. Understanding what it is like for her, and what you can do as a parent, is crucial. You have to understand what risk taking is and figure out the difference between healthy and unhealthy risks. Then you can guide your daughter as she learns.

Healthy Risks Versus Risky Behaviors

Not all risks are bad. Positive forms of risk taking include participating in sports, artistic and creative activities, volunteering, and even making new friends. In all of these activities, your daughter is testing new ground and finding out what she does and does not like, what she excels at, and where she feels comfortable. Undertaking any new endeavor represents a risk and can have positive results—improving her confidence and self-esteem or helping her better understand her own values.

As parents, we often have a keen eye for the dangerous risks our daughters may take, including using tobacco, alcohol, or other drugs. The dangers available today leave us wondering whether our daughters will make it through adolescence safely. Although we may expect our daughters to do some "innocent" experimentation, the truth is that even experimentation can evolve into more dangerous behaviors. Drinking, smoking, drug use, reckless driving, unsafe sexual activity, self-mutilation, running away, stealing,

> *"I think people my age turn to bad stuff because it relieves some of our worries for a while. Parents don't believe us, but we do have a lot of pressures. Things like drinking or drugs help us relax. All the other cool kids are doing it, too."*
> Age 13

gang activity, and disordered eating may start with experimentation but soon develop into dangerous risk taking, often complicated by psychological problems such as depression or anxiety. Girls give many reasons for taking these chances: they feel a natural need to push boundaries; they believe the activity will make them fit in with friends; and the exciting side of the dangers gives them an escape from depression or boredom.

Medicating Away Problems

When it comes to the use of illicit substances, girls' use of marijuana, LSD, cocaine, heroin, and inhalants is generally lower than boys'. Girls may use slightly more amphetamines (for weight control) and tranquilizers (usually for anxiety). Girls tend to begin experimenting with alcohol and drugs around ages 10 to 12, while boys begin experimenting at ages 12 to 14. Sixty percent of smokers start in the seventh grade or earlier.[1]

The fact that girls mature before boys, the easy availability of substances, and media portrayals of drug use and smoking all play roles in girls' use of dangerous substances. Rates of depression and anxiety are almost twice as high for adolescent girls as for boys, which can mean many girls are trying to medicate away those problems by using illicit substances. Cigarette companies are aware of this and design ads portraying tobacco as a form of mood management for women: note cigarette ads that show women

1. Ralph Diclemente, Larry Brown, and Lynn Ponton, *Handbook of Adolescent Health-Risk Behavior*, 2nd ed. (New York: Plenham Publishing, 2001).

laughing and frolicking with friends. If you discover your daughter is using alcohol or drugs, consider whether she could be trying to self-medicate. Look for these factors: has her concentration dropped off or irritability risen, or have her grades fallen? Has she mentioned a "friend" who has problems with these substances?

Generally, dangerous risks do not occur on their own—they appear in groups. For example, drinking and drug use frequently accompany unprotected sexual intercourse. Skipping school and running away from home are another pair regularly seen together. Be alert to clusters of risky behavior in your daughter— they are a red flag for danger.

"My friend and I found her parents' brandy, and she said, 'Hey, I'll distract my dad while you mix the Coke and brandy.' We ended up getting drunk. It was fun because she was my friend. But I guess I should be more careful, because if I drink around other people, I could get taken advantage of. If drinking becomes a normal habit, like at parties, then it is a potentially dangerous situation as far as rape goes."
Age 12

The Influence of Her Friends

For generations, we parents have wanted to believe that peers are the major influence on our child's decisions to smoke, drink, use drugs, or try other risky behaviors. It's easy to see why this idea is so attractive. If friends are the main influences on our daughter's risk taking, then our roles as parents are minimal. Recent studies indicate peer influence is related to earlier substance abuse, drinking, sexual debuts, and delinquency for boys and girls. But what makes up "peer pressure" is still unclear. Do kids try dangerous substances in order to conform to their peer group, or are kids who are already inclined to engage in risky behavior drawn together? We don't know.

We do know that many girls who are reluctant to take risks do so vicariously through friends. I've also seen girls in my office team up with "rebellious" boyfriends. These girls will not take risks themselves, but they take pleasure in their boyfriends' dangerous behavior. At the start, many girls do not see how easily they can be drawn into these behaviors. This is where you need to help your daughter explore risk taking in a healthy manner, instead of letting her live it through the lives of others. It may require helping your daughter see that she actually wants to be a risk taker.

Taking healthy risks can ward off peer pressure and offset the taking of dangerous risks. Help your daughter try things such as travel, sports, creative hobbies, and activities in which she can meet new groups of friends. These positive actions can help her feel good about herself, increasing her self-esteem so she can stand firm against her friends' influences. Not only do these activities remove your daughter from her current physical surroundings, but they also give her the courage to make her own choices.

Much of peer influence is based not so much on what your daughter's friends are actually doing but on what she thinks they are doing. Sometimes helping your daughter understand what is really happening with her friends can decrease her own unhealthy risk behaviors. Remind her, "It's important to some kids to impress others. Do you think your friend might be talking about things she hasn't actually done?" Or, "I used to have friends I really liked, but I knew I couldn't believe everything they said. I knew a lot of what they said was just talk."

Growing Up Faster

The many biological changes your daughter is coping with can influence her desire to try risky behaviors. Research shows that girls today are developing earlier than ever before; the onset of puberty now occurs on average two years earlier than it did 20 years ago. Girls who develop early often associate with older friends, which might help explain their earlier experiences with smoking, drugs, and drinking.

Girls who get their first menstrual period early—at age 9 or 10—are more vulnerable to dangerous risk taking during adolescence. They experiment with alcohol, tobacco, and drugs at earlier ages, have more struggles with eating, initiate sexual activity, and are less likely to have safer sex.[2] If your daughter engages in risky behavior early, she has less time to just be whole and happy and to learn to be herself within her new body.

It's Everywhere You Look

Popular culture—the Internet, television, videos, magazines, music, and film—is an increasing influence in girls' lives. Selectively chosen images of women's bodies are used to sell consumer goods. Our daughters are exposed daily to unrealistic images of bodies they will never be able to attain. Popular entertainment glamorizes views of young people drinking, smoking, and engaging in risky behavior. Some marketers of adult-oriented substances even discreetly try to capture the younger market.

If you discover your 10-, 11-, or 12-year-old daughter watching a movie in which young people smoke, drink, or use illicit substances, don't be surprised. Seize the opportunity to talk. Help her look beyond the surface and recognize the dangers that are portrayed. When you see young actresses smoking or drinking on television, talk with your daughter about the situations shown. Does the program make it seem as if the risky behavior will solve the

2. Laurence Steinberg, *Adolescence*, 5th ed. (New York: McGraw-Hill Higher Education, 1999).

girl's problem, make her feel better, or be more popular? Does the program portray stereotypical behavior—is it the "bad girl" or "cool girl" who smokes? Could that character really lead the exciting, active lifestyle shown if she was a chronic smoker or drinker? Would she really be as attractive to the cute male star if she smelled like cigarettes? Help your daughter see the hidden risks behind the behavior. Age-appropriate talks with her need to start when she is eight or nine years old.

We parents also need to examine our own attitudes about the media. One mother I worked with encouraged her daughter to adopt a critical attitude toward the media and advertising, but this mother continued to smoke in order to lose weight. The mother's behavior said more to her daughter than had all of their conversations.

Teaching Risk Assessment

Risk taking is part of American culture. Westward expansion and the settling of frontiers, including California, Alaska, and even space, were all risky ventures. The successful pursuit of "the American dream" requires risk taking, yet we neglect to teach our daughters how to assess risks, a skill they desperately need in adolescence. Without knowing how to evaluate risks, adolescents are likely to engage in dangerous behaviors without fully realizing their impact. As a result, boys and girls in the United States currently have the highest percentages of dangerous risk taking among teenagers in the western world.

We need to understand that risk taking is a vital part of life and that we should not prevent our children from taking all risks. Then we can shift our focus to helping our daughters assess risk in a healthier way. Ask questions that help your daughter understand what she is doing and why, such as, "Do you feel pressure from your friends to try _____ (drinking, smoking, drugs, or other behavior)?" "Do you ever feel you have to rush into these decisions instead of being able to think through the consequences?" "When you decide to try something you know is dangerous—like drugs, drinking, or smoking—does it ever feel like it is happening 'in a dream'?" If she feels as if it is in a dream, she is disconnected from her feelings. The goal is to help her recognize and connect with her feelings and, hopefully, to assess risk in a healthier way.

Do not bombard her with all of these questions at once; ask just one or two to help her begin to examine her choices. You can also try questions such as, "Does trying these things in front of others make you feel brave and strong?" "Does it feel more exciting to take a dangerous risk than to try things in a safe manner?"

Your daughter may tell you that she does not want to talk about smoking, drinking, or drug use, but right behind her statement you may sense her unspoken questions. Girls taking dangerous risks struggle with whether to tell their parents what they are doing. They are often afraid they will let their parents down or be judged harshly. Talking with your daughter nonjudgmentally about these subjects is important. It will be up to you to begin the conversation, but opening the door will give your daughter a forum to keep talking, and ultimately she will be able to better navigate her decisions.

> "I can't talk about drugs very well with my parents. They have pretty closed-minded views, so I am not sure how they would react to what I would say."
> age 13

More boys than girls are involved in risky behaviors. This may be because, generally, both mothers and fathers subtly promote risk taking in their sons. However, this also means boys are usually encouraged to participate in many positive challenges from which girls are discouraged. In some families, it is particularly difficult for us mothers—who have functioned as our daughters' protectors since they were in our wombs—to shift our focus and now encourage our daughters to take risks. Mothers may also find that they take few healthy risks themselves. One way to break free from this is for mothers and daughters to take risks together. Sign up together for a class in something neither of you has tried before. Or agree that each of you will try something you have been afraid of in the past—you will take horseback riding if your daughter will try a skiing lesson. Have a celebratory dinner when you've accomplished your goals.

Teach Her to Negotiate

More than a decade ago, I was asked to participate in designing a single-factor drug-prevention program, a type often referred to as "just say no." I refused. Why? Risk taking is complex. Many factors are involved, and today we know that "just say no" prevention programs have been largely unsuccessful. How do you get your daughter to say "no" appropriately when you know that simply telling her to do so does not work? By teaching her to successfully voice her own opinion.

This can be an important first step, and it is not an easy thing for some girls to do. Girls often want to avoid conflict, be liked by everyone, and fit in. They struggle with saying "no" even if they know it is in their own best interest, and so they find it especially difficult to negotiate risky situations. You can encourage your daughter to build negotiating skills in all situations, not only those that are life-and-death. Role-play a situation in which you take turns playing a friend trying to get your daughter to try drinking, smoking, or drugs. Or have her play a friend being tempted to try these things. With this practice under her belt, she will be better able to express and negotiate her own desires, and that is an important part of mastering risk taking and life in general.

Dr. Lynn Ponton is the author of **The Romance of Risk: Why Teenagers Do the Things They Do** *and* **The Sex Lives of Teenagers.** *She is a psychoanalyst, a professor at the University of California at San Francisco, and the mother of two teenage daughters. She has worked with teenagers and their parents for more than 20 years.*

LISTENING IN

Dr. Ponton looks at what to do when girls test their limits with cigarettes, alcohol, and other drugs.

"Peer pressure doesn't bother me."

"A couple of my friends have tried to get me to smoke cigarettes with them. I told them I really wasn't into stinky breath, yellow teeth, and lung cancer."

Age 13

Dr. Ponton: In a few words, this girl is able to communicate that smoking is unhealthy and, in some ways, disgusting. Her letter helps us understand the power of practicing responses with our daughters so that they can answer their peers' suggestions quickly and firmly. It also helps us understand how much appearance matters to young girls.

When you practice comebacks at home with a young daughter, keep the responses light in tone, focused on appearance, and without a heavy emotional or moral flavor. It is likely that she hears warnings about lung cancer and emphysema at school, and she is more likely to respond to warnings of side effects that would hit home now, not at some time in the distant future. An older girl will be able to weave her values and morals into her response.

"My friends and I made a promise never to do anything that could hurt our bodies, because we don't know what we would do without each other."

Age 11

Dr. Ponton: This girl is only 11 years old, but her letter shows how significant peer support is among young girls. Her friendship pact is very important and indicates that peer support can help girls say "no" to smoking, drinking, and drugs. She tells us how meaningful relationships are to all girls when she says "we don't know what we would do without each other." Like many girls, feeling connected to others is a motivator for her, as it probably is for your daughter.

"I've been asked to do drugs, and I have declined. I'm not that stupid. I have big dreams and high goals for myself, and those things would only hold me back. My friends and I don't do that kind of stuff, but

I think other teens turn to drugs, drinking, and such things to get away from their problems. I know that is the wrong approach. Me, I like to write. I write about what I feel and why I feel it. Writing is my escape."

Age 14

Dr. Ponton: High goals keep this girl from trying drugs. One of her interests, writing, is a good example of a healthy type of risk taking. It allows her to express her feelings and "escape." If your daughter expends energy taking healthy risks, her self-esteem can increase and she will be less likely to take unhealthy risks. Activities that encourage self-expression, such as writing, acting, or doing artwork, are particularly valuable because they help a girl discover who she is and what she wants to do. In turn, that helps her to withstand peer pressure.

"I've smoked or used drugs."

"I can't stop smoking cigarettes. It's such a bad habit! I want to quit so badly, because I know how much it can hurt me. I need help figuring out how to stop."

Age 10

Dr. Ponton: It is important to begin talking about the dangers of smoking when your daughter is eight or nine years old, because for most girls, experimentation occurs at age ten, eleven, or twelve. Addiction to cigarettes, alcohol, or drugs can occur at any age. If you discover your daughter has a problem, discuss treatment options with her. There are programs tailored just for teens; they often involve group treatment, use of a nicotine patch for tobacco addiction, and other medications to treat anxiety and side effects of withdrawal. Although addiction is a serious problem for young girls, early intervention helps, especially if it is followed by periodic checkups and further treatment if needed. Your daughter's pediatrician, a specialist in adolescent medicine, and a school counselor are good resources to help you with treatment options and programs.

If you or members of your family smoke, drink, or use illegal substances, think about the effect this has on your daughter. Parents often worry about the influence of their daughter's friends, but they fail to discuss or even hide their own involvement in these activities. Honestly answering your daughters' questions and seeking treatment

if you need it can help your daughter make better choices in this rocky area.

"My best friend and I got together one day in the woods near this creek. We spent a few hours there just sitting, talking, and smoking weed. It was an awesome day. We were able to just mellow out and be together. I think people should be able to use drugs more freely, because when used responsibly, they can be very good. Also, if someone chooses to use them irresponsibly and dies, then it is her fault."
Age 14

Dr. Ponton: Adolescents often see situations in black and white, failing to see the many shades of gray. Experimentation is certainly a part of adolescence, and this girl is clearly aware of some of the risks of using marijuana or other drugs. When you share your disapproval of something like drug use with your daughter, do so carefully. Remember that during this phase of life you are a guide, not a cop. If she has confided in you about how she feels, you might begin, "I appreciate your ideas, but you need to think about the risk you are placing yourself in." You would then discuss legality—including

arrest and potential expulsion from school because of zero-tolerance policies—health concerns, and potential addictions. It is best to have several conversations and not pack this into one judgmental talk.

It is easy for this girl to distance herself from the frightening consequences of what she terms irresponsible drug use. *That can't happen to me,* she thinks. Helping our daughters understand and assess risks involves a comprehension of not only extremes but also the gray zone in between.

Yet, helping your daughter discern the gray zone in most areas of life is often frustrating. You can make the conversation less personal by discussing situations in the media that highlight morals or values. Explain your own thinking, but do not feel rejected if she rolls her eyes at you in response. Adolescence is a time when girls are struggling to determine their own values. They often do not like to hear about yours, even if your point of view includes an expression of understanding. But take heart: daughters remember what their parents have said when they are experimenting.

"I've tried the drug Ecstasy, I'm sad to say. It made me feel good, but that feeling can get out of control if you aren't careful. The one time I tried pot, I had the worst experience. I was with an ex-boyfriend, and I felt sick, and I just wanted to go to sleep. He was all over me, trying to kiss me and be romantic, and all I wanted to do was throw up."

Age unknown

Dr. Ponton: This girl writes about a whole range of risky behaviors and highlights the connection between illicit substances and unwanted sexual activity. It is important for our daughters to know that over half of the sexual experiences had by girls under age 15 involve drinking or illicit substance use.[3]

Sharing just cold statistics may not bring home the message, however, so put it in terms she can understand. You might try words such as, "Here's what can happen if you use drugs or drink when you're in a social situation with boys. You're having fun at a party, you have a few drinks or try a drug that someone's brought, and things start to feel good. Everyone's jokes seem very funny. A guy starts to put moves on you and, because of the drugs or alcohol, you don't resist as much as you would if you were sober. You may think you know what you're doing at the time, but it's not until later you realize that you just said 'Yes' to a guy you would have said 'No' to any other time."

Let her know that boys often try to see how far they can push a girl's limits when she's not sober. Knowing that sexual activity and using illicit substances are connected can help our daughters make better choices. This is a message girls really need to hear.

"Do you want to know why we take these risks?"

"The reason I do drugs is because I live in a very small, very boring town, and there's nothing else to do. Most of my friends and I do drugs, although I wouldn't say we have serious problems."

Age 14

Dr. Ponton: This girl's letter underscores an important point. If healthy risk-taking alternatives are not provided for teens, they will find their own options, and dangerous risks such as drugs are certainly among them.

3. Ralph Diclemente, Larry Brown, and Lynn Ponton, *Handbook of Adolescent Health-Risk Behavior*, 2nd ed. (New York: Plenham Publishing, 2001).

Parents often need to actively seek out opportunities for their daughters. If sports or the arts are not to your daughter's taste, volunteer work or a part-time job can also provide stimulating experiences. A small town is often a challenge for activity-starved girls. Sharing ideas with other parents in the same area can lead you to more options. You might start a mother-daughter book group, do a group charity project, or organize a trip. The best way to help a daughter find areas of interest is to present her with interesting choices.

"I think people turn to drugs to show that they need love. The drugs fill the place in them that they feel is empty."
Age unknown
Dr. Ponton: This girl's view is simplistic, but in my experience, at least a part of all girls' substance use involves trying to find love or fill up some place in themselves. If you hear this message from your daughter, it is crucial to reach out to her about her about feelings of emptiness. Be aware that opening up to other trusted adults or a therapist can also help her get to the heart of her loneliness. Lastly, turn up the volume on the mes-

sages of warmth, affection, and unconditional acceptance you send your daughter every day.

"I think smoking bidis is a way teens get themselves used to smoking more powerful drugs. They are widely used, easier to get hold of, and less expensive than many other illegal drugs teens use today."
Age 15
Dr. Ponton: Bidis are flavored cigarettes from India that come in colorful packages and are currently popular with girls. Many consumers think they are harmless; in truth, because they are unfiltered they deliver more toxins than traditional cigarettes. Teenagers also find bidis appealing because they aren't sold in mainstream culture. Smoking them can make your daughter feel exotic and rebellious. Talk with her about cigarette alternatives like bidis and clove cigarettes, and let her know they are as dangerous as traditional cigarettes.

"Someone I care about has a drug-abuse problem."
"My mom is an alcoholic, and I worry too much about her. Sometimes when I have a choice to go somewhere either with my mom or

my dad, I choose my dad because I think my mom will have been drinking. When I leave with him, I feel guilty for hurting my mom's feelings. My dad tells me not to worry, but I still do."
Age unknown

Dr. Ponton: The daughter of a parent with a substance-abuse problem almost always struggles with difficult and complex feelings. This girl feels guilty when she chooses to be with her dad rather than her mother. She might feel too much pain or responsibility when she is with her mother. She might also be afraid for her or fearful of her. Conflict, guilt, pain, and sometimes denial are unfortunate legacies that alcohol and substance abusers leave to their children.

This girl's father is trying to help her feel less pain by telling her not to worry. If you are a nondrinker in a relationship with an alcoholic, help your daughter understand that she is not responsible for her alcoholic parent's drinking. Do not be afraid to seek additional help. Therapy and teen versions of support groups like Al-Anon are helpful; a spouse who denies the alcoholic parent's problem is not.

"Talking to my parents helps."
"I've talked with my parents about the whole drug issue, and I know their feelings toward it. All of our discussions have been pretty casual. Even so, I still take everything they say to heart, and these conversations definitely have an impact on me."
Age 13

Dr. Ponton: These parents are on the right track. By keeping discussions with their daughter informal and not confrontational, their message is hitting home. If you start your talks before your daughter is experimenting, you can lay groundwork for relaxed conversations that will be helpful when you come back to the subject as she ages. As your conversations develop, be prepared for what you will hear. If you want her to be honest about her habits, do not attack her when she confesses she has already tried drinking or smoking. Try to respond calmly. The key is to find out what feelings the smoking, drinking, or drug use mask. Tune in to why she is experimenting, who else is present when she does, and what else is going on in her life. If you understand her reasons for using a substance, you can better understand how to encourage her to quit.

YOUR ROLE

Remember that it's not about you. An unhealthy risk may appear to be an angry gesture directed at you, but most often it is part of your daughter's search for her own identity. That does not mean you should turn a blind eye; stay involved and provide guidance.

Talk safety and consequences. Be clear about your family's guidelines regarding drinking, smoking, and drug use. Be frank about the consequences your daughter will face if she breaks the rules.

Know the facts about smoking and weight loss. Girls often smoke to control their weight. If your daughter does this, help her understand the addiction that might already be forming, and, if necessary, support her in healthy methods of weight loss.

Share facts about alcohol. Teach your daughter that girls don't metabolize alcohol at the same rate boys do. If a girl and boy who are the same weight drink the same amount of alcohol, the alcohol moves out of the girl's bloodstream more slowly than it moves out of the boy's. The girl gets drunk faster and stays that way longer.

Talk about your own experiences. Frank discussion about what you have learned can help your daughter better evaluate risks and consequences. Admitting you know about the lures of cigarettes or illicit substances may help her absorb your advice, especially if she uses substances daily or is a binge user (using large quantities at a time, less frequently).

Learn about cessation programs. If your daughter is a regular or binge user of risky substances, talk with her about cessation programs. Do your research, and let her know the options. Communicate that it is easier to stop now than later.

Look in the mirror. If you smoke, drink, or engage in other risky behaviors, get help for yourself before you talk with your daughter.

Teach coping skills. If your daughter learns to use substances to deal with stress or fear, her ability to develop real coping skills can be compromised. Teach her forms of stress relief, problem-solving strategies, and ways to overcome nervousness in social situations.

Have faith in her. Teach your daughter your values, then stand back. With alcohol, for example, after a period of experimentation the majority of girls grow up to be young women who drink moderately or not at all.

Dating and Sexuality

by Lynn Ponton, M.D.

"My friends have boyfriends, and I want one, too. I know that doesn't sound right, but I'm serious. I want this one boy to like me. How should I find out if he is interested? Should I ask him out? I don't know how to handle this situation."

age 11

"I worry when I see girls online talking about how far they have gone with boys. Some have even had sex at the age of 12. Even at 18, they would be too young to be doing that stuff. When I was 12, I barely had breasts! Besides, there's enough in life to worry about at those ages—why add another issue?"

Age 14

Thinking about romance and relationships—and experimenting with them—is an important part of life for adolescent girls. Our introductory letters show us the extremes that can exist between young girls and where they are in "boy world." Some girls are just beginning to feel romantic attractions. They have crushes and seem to talk endlessly with friends about the daily activities of boys they know or want to know. They may go on casual group outings with boys and girls. Or they may be satisfied to keep romance confined to daydreams.

Other girls may be uninterested in boys, even though all their friends are entangled in who-likes-who romantic intrigues. And, as the second introductory letter points out, still other girls progress more quickly, having sexual relationships for which they may not be ready. This process of discovery—both good and bad—helps a girl develop her sexual identity, a vital part of her overall identity. It is not just our daughters who must be prepared to deal with the emotional and physical issues involving boys, romance, and dating; we parents have to adapt and be ready to support our daughters so that they can learn to develop healthy, balanced, loving relationships throughout their lives.

The Road to Romance

Girls are thinking about boys and their own sexuality at young ages. Like many of our daughters, the girl in our first letter is unsure of what to do. She appears to have courage and she's certainly curious about how having a boyfriend works. Her parents should have supportive conversations with her about socializing with boys, feeling sure of herself, and maintaining her identity when she's in a relationship. They can help her learn not to base her self-esteem on whether or not she has a boyfriend.

When your daughter first becomes interested in boys, along with the hearts-and-flowers emotions of her first crush, you may see her struggle with her lack of experience, almost impossible expectations, and

"I can't stop thinking about boys. I try to put them out of my head, but five minutes later, I'm thinking about them again!"
Age 11

confusion about what she feels or wants. At this stage, her interest in boys is not about sex; she's thinking about romance, idealized boyfriends, and that dreamy moment of her first kiss.

> *"Being 14 years old is hard enough without having to deal with the consequences of sex. When I am older and in love, I will decide for myself if I'm ready. I think some girls and guys don't understand what can happen to a relationship after you have intercourse."*
> age 14

A girl's confusion and changing emotions are normal parts of figuring out who she is and what she wants out of life. As you help her find answers, remember that girls often get the impression that as soon as their bodies begin developing, they should be ready for sexual activity. Help your daughter learn that she can stay on a safe middle ground—where she can be interested in boys and romance without being sexually active. Being ready for romance does not mean she is ready for intercourse.

Your daughter may have reached the stage at which boyfriends have become the "in thing" among her friends. This is not surprising; unfortunately, it is strongly accepted in our culture that girls need relationships with boys in order to be okay. Many girls watch their mothers struggle with being alone, or listen to a father ask why they don't date. If you underscore to your daughter that her value is not based on her relationships with boys, you will counter the "boy craziness" and encourage her to look within—not to the opposite sex—for help in defining herself and feeling good about herself.

Boyfriends as Status Symbols

Relationships do provide status for teens and adults, but you can teach your daughter that good relationships are about far more than that. Point out positive aspects of relationships among the couples you observe in daily life. When you highlight the companionship, sharing, and trust you see in couples you know, you help your daughter understand why relationships are truly valuable, and you teach her what she should look for in her own dates.

If your daughter thinks having a boyfriend will help her fit in, she may begin putting aside her own needs in order to please a boy or keep him around. Teach her not to be passive and to keep a balance of power in any friendship—whether with a boy or a girl. She should not hesitate to say "no" to a boy because she is afraid of hurting his feelings or embarrassing him, or because she thinks the boy has a right to be aggressive. Let her know that "yes" and "no" are not a game. Tell her, "You need to tell your date 'no' when you mean 'no' and 'yes' when you mean 'yes.' And let him know you mean what you say." There should be no gray area here.

> *"My boyfriend of a few days and I were watching a rented movie. We held hands, but then he moved my hand toward his private parts. I didn't like touching him one bit. It was a stupid thing to do, but I felt like I had to do it because we were going out, and I had already let him touch my breast. I thought he wouldn't like me anymore if I didn't. I felt trapped. I don't know how to refuse, because I'm shy and not good at standing up for myself."*
> Age 14

Sexual Activity

As your daughter moves into adolescence, she may begin thinking about sex even if she is not talking about it. Indeed, when our daughters are between the ages of 10 and 14, the bulk of their sexual activity occurs in fantasy. It is normal that some girls masturbate and others do not. Respecting your daughter's privacy is vital here. It is neither necessary nor healthy for parents to be "in on" a daughter's fantasies, but it is important to not make her feel shame about her sexual feelings.

Girls start puberty earlier than boys, so be prepared. Your daughter may have a curvy, adult-looking body at age 12 or 13, and she may face sexual attention long before she is ready to

> *"I was proud of myself when I stopped this guy from touching me someplace I didn't want him to touch. It made me really uncomfortable, because we weren't dating and I only think of him as a friend. I felt proud because I told him to stop it and leave me alone. Usually I would just try to get away without saying anything, but this time he really made me mad."*
>
> age 14

deal with it. Guide her through the inappropriate attention she might receive. Teach her comebacks ("I'm only 11, even though I look older") and encourage her to talk to you and other supportive adults.

When it comes to having intercourse, the statistics are alarming. Studies show that 50 percent of girls report having sexual intercourse by age 16. Large numbers of girls describe feeling afraid during their first sexual experience (63 percent in one study). One study found that 74 percent of girls who had intercourse before age 14—and 60 percent who had it by age 15—felt forced into it.[1]

Communicate gently but honestly with your daughter about the psychological and emotional repercussions of having intercourse. Girls who have early intercourse often feel exploited, or used, or have a sense of having lost control—especially if they felt forced into the act. Discuss the false expectations a girl may feel: that she must have intercourse to please a boy, or that it will make him like her more, want to be her boyfriend, or inspire a new devotion or commitment from him. Talk about how deeply painful it can be to participate in such an intimate act and then not have these expectations met. Some girls treat sex as a commodity, using it to trade for status, popularity, and affection. Help your daughter see that if she has intercourse—or participates in any sexual act—for these reasons, it can cause her harm and pain instead of pleasure.

1. L. Neinstein and A. Nelson, "Contraception," in *Adolescent Health Care* (New York: Williams and Wilkins, 1996).

Dating Guidelines

Every family's beliefs and value systems are different, but these guidelines can help you decide what is right for your daughter's situation.

Don't push. There's no right age to begin dating, so don't worry if your daughter is not doing so. Some girls don't date until age 17 or 18.

Let her start with group dating. Girls feel less pressured on group outings where they can have the support of friends. Every girl is different, but 13 or 14 is an appropriate age for group dates in public places. Don't be afraid to chaperone.

Decide on an age for her first one-on-one date, and stick to it. While there are no hard and fast rules, age 15 or 16 is right for many girls. Be sure to explain your reasoning to your daughter.

Be available by telephone. Whether she's on group or solo outings, be sure she can contact you if she needs to.

Encourage her to date boys near her own age. Dating boys more than two years older or younger can result in a power imbalance and is associated with riskier behavior.

Set curfews. Get her input. She may still push against the chosen time, but her curfew is a safety net that lets her know she is protected. You are helping her learn important refusal skills and giving her an out if she's being pushed to do something she doesn't want to do.

Include the boyfriend in family activities. You'll get to know him. In addition, seeing him in ordinary situations takes him off the pedestal your daughter may have him on and puts them on more equal footing.

Reinforce her voice. Help her see her own power in a relationship. After a date, ask, "Did you help decide where you went and what you did? Did you two negotiate? How did it feel? Did you feel listened to?"

Starting at age 16, girls in the United States rank higher than girls in other industrialized countries when it comes to sexually risky behaviors such as unprotected intercourse and exposure to sexually transmitted disease. The rates of contracting the human immunodeficiency virus (HIV), which causes AIDS—acquired immune deficiency syndrome—are higher in the U.S. than in other industrialized nations.[2]

Many of us find it difficult to recognize that our adolescent daughters are struggling with graphic and shocking aspects of sexuality earlier than ever, so we ignore it. But how we handle this information and guide our daughters is crucial. Educate yourself about the risks your daughter faces and learn about the protective measures that are available—then prepare to tell her what you've learned.

You can communicate morals and values best by example, so be aware of how you speak and act in front of your daughter, even if you think she is not paying attention. Find out what sexual education your daughter is receiving in school; many teachers welcome parental input. There are other sources of sexual education besides school. Many youth organizations offer programs for girls. Health-care providers such as pediatricians and specialists in adolescent medicine are also available for consultation.

Having "Those" Talks

As your daughter gets older, your ability to converse about tough and often embarrassing subjects should also be improving. We all know that talking about sex is not easy, and there's no reason not to admit it! You can tell your daughter, "Sex is a personal topic and

2. Alan Guttmacher Institute Staff, *Sex and America's Teenagers* (New York: Alan Guttmacher Institute, 1994).

it's a little hard for me to talk about. Bear with me if I get embarrassed." Contrary to what some parents think, having a sexually explicit conversation with your daughter will not cause her to become sexually active. Research shows that girls who have close, open relationships with their parents delay intercourse longer, and they make responsible, healthy decisions overall.[3]

In her adolescent years, your daughter may not ask you direct questions about boys but may instead tell you stories about her "friend's" problems or situations. You can help by listening and showing interest. She will probably discount some of your comments as being out of date, but your willing ear is what's important. Months later, you may

> *"I'm not sexually active but I have been pressured, and I have almost given in on more than one occasion. But I always see my mother's face. I guess all her talks came in handy."*
> Age 14

overhear her repeating your "out-of-date" stories or advice to a friend, so be persistent. Your ability to listen to her validates that her stories are worth telling.

When you talk, be clear about your family's values and moral beliefs concerning sexual activity. Make sure your daughter understands the risks of unprotected sex and sexually transmitted diseases and knows about birth control. Let her know that young girls can be even more susceptible to sexually transmitted diseases because their cervixes are not yet mature. Discuss the messages about sexuality that you both see in the media. Be honest and open. Explore the language she hears outside the home and educate her on correct and respectful terminology. Use specific language yourself, even if it's hard to get the words out sometimes. Try not to say "sex" or "making love" if you mean intercourse,

3. *National Longitudinal Study of Adolescent Health* (University of Minnesota, 1998).

or "making out" if you mean kissing or touching.

Whatever her age, start talking now. Let your daughter know there are many rumors about sex that aren't true. Try words such as, "There's a lot of false information out there about sex, and I want you to know you can ask me if you have any questions." Or, "You can ask me anything and I'll try to answer you honestly." Don't be afraid to admit that you don't know all the answers. If you work together to find them, you show her that curiosity is nothing to be ashamed of. If you wait to address sex until your daughter is a teenager, and then frame it only in terms of fears and prohibitions (for example, warning of the risks of pregnancy or disease), it will be nearly impossible to develop reasonable communication. The topics you discuss will shift as your daughter matures, of course, but it will be much easier to address her personal choices about sexual activity when she is older if you have already had direct talks.

From television, ads, and movies, your daughter can get the idea that everyone is having and enjoying sex. She may not learn that sex can affect her deepest emotions and self-esteem. In real life she finds out that many sexual topics are labeled taboo. She faces a lack of meaningful communication and factual information. She will not be able to navigate these mysterious waters without your help. If you can create a climate in your home where she can talk openly and lovingly with you, she will be better able to face both the confusing and exciting issues that relationships bring.

Dr. Lynn Ponton is the author of **The Romance of Risk: Why Teenagers Do the Things They Do** *and* **The Sex Lives of Teenagers.** *She is a psychoanalyst, a professor at the University of California at San Francisco, and the mother of two teenage daughters. She has worked with teenagers and their parents for more than 20 years.*

LISTENING IN

Dr. Ponton sheds light on all levels of dating issues—from first crushes to breakups, harassment, and sexual activity.

"I'm not always sure how to deal with boys."

"This boy in my class has a crush on me, but I have no feelings for him. He asked me to slow dance, and he's starting to corner me at school. He is always looking over my shoulder and following me. It's making me feel uncomfortable, but I'm afraid to tell him to stop because I'm friends with his sister. I'm afraid I'll lose her as a friend."
Age 10

Dr. Ponton: Although the writer says she has "no feelings" for this boy, it appears she has many. The important first step is that she has recognized her own feelings of discomfort. Your job is to help her learn to express them. Tell her that her feelings are very important and that it's important she pay attention to them. Then encourage her to practice different responses to unwanted attention, such as: "Stop bothering me—I don't like you"; "I want to be your friend, but the way you are acting makes me uncomfortable"; or, to her female friend, "I want to be friends with your brother, but some of the things he is doing are not cool." Encourage your daughter to role-play different approaches with you until you find one that feels most comfortable to her.

After she practices her response at home and then tries it with the boy, it is time for Part Two of your discussion. How did it feel to tell him how she felt? What did she learn? What, if anything, would she do differently next time? Keep in mind that she may have to talk with the boy again, and you may want to repeat your practice session. There is no skill more valuable than the ability to express her feelings directly.

"I'm white and I like a boy who is black. He likes me, too. But sometimes I wonder if it is wrong to like him, because he's black. Will we have a breakup?"
Age 11

Dr. Ponton: Girls often worry that any sort of differences between themselves and a love interest or crush make a relationship "wrong."

If your daughter has similar fears, she needs to be listened to. Why does she think that liking a particular boy might be "wrong"? Do you share her concerns? How might you support her? What do you want to share with her about your own beliefs and experience?

Remember that she is young. Liking a boy, even "going together," might mean that they are only smiling at each other across the room. Find out how she defines the term "liking," and keep the conversations going.

"I met this great guy on the Internet, and he is perfect for me in every way. I saw his name one day and just personal-messaged him. He turned out to be the sweetest guy I had ever met. He understands me, helps me, and makes me feel good about myself. This relationship is different than with other guys I know, because I can talk to him about anything and he understands. I feel awkward sometimes with people I talk to face-to-face. My parents won't let me give him detailed information about me, but I don't mind. I don't really want to tell him that stuff, and he hasn't asked me for it anyway. I really, truly do trust him."
Age 13

Dr. Ponton: A shy girl can acquire greater ease with relationships by conversing with other boys and girls online. Shy teens are spared the face-to-face encounters that they fear because they believe so much depends on appearance, an area in which almost all adolescents feel insecure.

Although Internet relationships can be positive self-esteem builders for girls, they also pose problems and dangers. Without face-to-face contact, these relationships are often idealized. The friend online is seen as perfect. Blemishes—physical or otherwise—can be hidden easily in cyberspace. Clearly, meeting an online friend in person can be dangerous. He may not be the age or even the gender he says he is, so parents are right to limit the disclosure of information to him (presumably the girl's full name, phone number, and address). If an in-person meeting were to take place, it would need to be carefully thought out with parents actively involved.

"Other girls are boy crazy."
"I've been best friends with this girl for three years, but she's changed. Now that she has a boyfriend, it's like I'm not even here. We used to

do everything together. My other friends all have boyfriends, too. I feel left out."
Age 11

Dr. Ponton: Often, a girl between the ages of 10 and 13 becomes upset when she discovers that what she thinks or feels about romance or dating doesn't fit with what her friends believe. This girl's relationship with her best friend has changed now that the other girl has a boyfriend. In our letter writer's mind, she no longer exists in this friend's world.

If your daughter is in a similar bind, counsel her that she will have to spend time with other friends or find ways to adapt to this unsatisfactory situation. Provide emotional support and help her seek out other friends and activities so that she doesn't feel so left out.

"I am a devout Christian. I'm only 13 and I have never gone out with a guy or even thought of dating. Some people criticize me for my decisions, but that's the way I feel. I guess I am pretty critical of girls who make the choice to date. I hear about 11-year-olds bragging about their boyfriends, and they almost flaunt it like a status symbol. It's

usually because everyone else has a boyfriend. It just makes me want to yell at them, 'You're still a kid! You shouldn't have to worry about this stuff!' "
Age 13

Dr. Ponton: This girl is confident about her own beliefs. Girls from devout religious backgrounds tend to delay sexual activity one to two years longer than do their peers. This girl understands that many girls seek boyfriends for the wrong reasons—in her words, as status symbols. She recognizes that 11-year-olds are still kids. If your daughter voices views like these, let her know you are proud of her independence and support her desire to move at her own pace.

"He's *not* my boyfriend."
"I have a good friend who's a boy, and our parents think we're boyfriend and girlfriend. It's totally not true. Once we wanted to go to the mall together with some other friends and my parents said, 'No, you can't date.' We just wanted to be with our friends and have fun. I don't know what to do."
Age 11

Dr. Ponton: It is okay for girls and boys to be friends and hang out together. In general, Americans

push girls and boys into dating relationships long before they are ready for them.

A group activity among boys and girls is not a bad idea, for platonic friends or otherwise. You can drop a group of young people at the mall and sit and have a cup of coffee. It allows the kids time with friends of the opposite sex outside of a date and gives you a chance to observe the mall scene. You can see if it is the way your daughter describes it—"just kids having fun"—or if something else is happening.

"I got into the whole trust issue with my parents when I wanted to go to my guy friend's house when his parents weren't home. I thought my parents didn't trust me, but they said they didn't trust the guy. They brought up this time when I went there and didn't tell them his parents were gone. I would have told them, but they didn't ask."
Age 14

Dr. Ponton: Poor communication is the theme in this letter. The parents tell their daughter they trust her but don't trust the boy, giving her a message that she is not as responsible as he is for what happens. The writer also lets

us know she is not giving her parents any more information than they ask for.

In such a situation, strive to talk more openly with your daughter, starting with "Let me share why I was uncomfortable with you being at your friend's house without his parents home." Then practice what she should do the next time she arrives and discovers his parents are out. Let her know that you would like her to call you immediately if this happens, and also to let the boy know that his parents need to be at home when she visits. Continue to have conversations about trust and related issues.

"Is it enough to just be myself?"
"I am usually really shy. But I overheard my crush saying he likes wild girls, not shy, nerdy ones. So a couple of popular girls said I should criticize my best friend's new haircut. I did it so he would think I was in the popular group. My friend cried and ran to the bathroom. I felt really bad afterwards, and I talked to her about it. Luckily, she forgave me. I no longer try to fit in with people that aren't my type."
Age 13

Dr. Ponton: This girl is trying to decide how much she should

change, if at all, in order to attract a boy. There is pressure to do this because, in part, many people still feel a girl's worth is based on her appearance and the boys she can attract. Exactly who a girl *is* can get lost, especially if this pressure starts at ages 10, 11, and 12— the years when she is beginning the important process of identity formation. If she doesn't learn defenses, she can fall into a pattern of morphing for a boy, putting her own interests aside, and losing the sense of self that can make her strong. Recognize that your daughter can be easily pulled in this direction and work to support her struggles for her own identity. Encourage her to participate in activities that will help her feel capable, talented, and popular *without* a boy at her side.

"How far is too far?"

"My friends and I sometimes play Truth or Truth in an online chat room, and a lot of questions have to do with how far you would go sexually. I am uncomfortable talking about that with people who may not be good friends, especially guys, so most of the time I keep my mouth shut. At this point, the farthest I'd go is making out. My friend went to second base with a guy, and I didn't approve. I told her my feelings about it, but we're still friends."
Age 13

Dr. Ponton: Most parents need to recognize that their daughters are more experienced on the Internet than they are. Although this girl knows how to find her way into chat rooms, she understands that she doesn't know a whole lot about sex yet. She desires information. If your daughter has access to the Internet, increase the number of conversations you have about what goes on online. This girl is already 13; with a younger daughter, protective measures such as V-chips can be installed in the computer to block sexually explicit language online. At 13, the best "prevention" is an open conversation with your daughter.

"I mistakenly got involved with a guy who was three years older than I was. He would constantly pressure me to give him oral sex. Finally I gave in, feeling that I would lose him if I didn't. I thought that would be a tragic loss, because at the time I thought he was all I had. I thought if

*I said no it would be the end of
everything."*
Age 14

Dr. Ponton: The rate of oral sex is
rising among 10- to 14-year-old
girls. Many classify oral sex with
masturbation and believe it is
harmless, a commonly held myth.
Let your daughter know that oral
sex carries the risk of sexually
transmitted diseases, including
HIV. Many girls also discount the
emotional baggage that can go
along with it. Teach your daughter
to take this seriously by saying
something like, "There are many
steps in sexual activity. Oral sex
isn't intercourse, but it is still
powerful and emotional and can
affect your relationship. You need
to be ready to deal with it."

Sadly, many young girls fail
to appreciate their own value and
simultaneously overvalue boyfriends they don't think they can
live without. It's important to rid
your daughter of the belief that she
must find her primary worth in
romantic relationships. Luckily,
this girl is already in the process of
changing her attitude about this,
and support from a parent will help.

*"Every day at school, boys make fun
of my body. I sit down off to the side,*
*but they still keep talking, even
though they know it hurts and
embarrasses me. What should I say?"*
Age unknown

Dr. Ponton: Agreement about what
constitutes sexual harassment of
girls is changing as we see how
frequently it is occurring in middle
schools, high schools, and now
even in elementary schools. The
Equal Employment Opportunity
Commission defines sexual harassment as unwelcome sexual attention. The state of Minnesota has
some of the most well-developed
guidelines, defining sexual harassment to include grabbing, bra-
snapping, spreading sexual rumors,
pressuring a student for dates,
making gestures associated with
masturbation or sexual intercourse,
sharing sexually explicit written
material, and making verbal comments such as teasing about body
development, sexual activity, or
name-calling.

What this girl has experienced
is indeed sexual harassment. It
can cause deep pain both for the
victim and for her loving parents.
If your daughter experiences
harassment, your first step is to
let her know you empathize with
the hurt, embarrassment, and confusion she might be feeling. Next,

let her know that harassment is not acceptable, even if the boys—or other girls—laugh it off. Help her determine what is bothering her most about the boys' actions. It might be helpful to have an adult mediate when she confronts the boy or boys about their behavior. Although confronting a harasser often helps a girl feel stronger, it does not necessarily change the boy's behavior. Generally, teachers have to get involved and work hard to stop it. It often may be part of a widespread pattern in the school.

"I've been wondering about sex."

"I've been having a lot of thoughts about sex lately. They make me uncomfortable. How can I get rid of bad thoughts?"

Age unknown

Dr. Ponton: This girl is uncomfortable just having thoughts about sex and probably feels they are abnormal. She would feel better if she understood that such thoughts are natural and that they don't mean she has to, or should, act on them. If you find out your daughter feels this way, talk with her about what she feels is "bad." Does she believe any thoughts about sex are wrong or just certain ones? Most likely she will not share her specific thoughts, but you can volunteer that thoughts and even elaborate day and night dreams that focus on sex are a normal part of growing up.

"I am 11, and the boys in my class are pressuring me to have sex. I don't know what to do."

Age 11

Dr. Ponton: When girls say "sex," it is important to understand how they use the term. This girl leaves us wondering. She already feels pressured by boys to have "sex," but she is not specific about what that means. Is she being teased, harassed, or seriously pressured to participate in fondling, touching, or even intercourse? Girls are feeling this type of pressure at earlier ages, so it is unfortunately no surprise to me that this writer is only 11.

As parents, you need to be aware of this pressure, and you *will* be if you listen to your daughter and ask questions. Does she feel put down by the boys' comments? Does she have comebacks ready? Does she feel okay talking to a teacher when boys pressure her? Is she secretly flattered by the attention? If so, help her see that harassment is not a compliment—it's wrong. A supportive, nonjudgmental attitude is vital. Encourage her to keep talking with you about it.

"I have been hanging out with a new girl at school. Ever since then, I have been having sexual feelings and fantasies about her. Would I be considered a lesbian?"
Age 13

Dr. Ponton: Forty percent of adolescent girls experience erotic attraction for other girls during their adolescence. It is normal and does not necessarily indicate homosexuality. Some girls are attracted to a best friend, and others to a girl they know only slightly, if at all. The factors that determine sexual orientation are complex. Although the causes are not yet known, most researchers believe basic sexual orientation is established at an early age, with both biology and environment playing a role.

If your daughter expresses similar thoughts, try not to overreact. Recognize that her feelings are fluid, not to mention confusing, at this point. What she needs from you is the support she may not be able to give herself. Your reaction is important; one study showed

that a lack of acceptance from parents was the most common reason homosexual youth attempt suicide.

While you may want a direct answer to the question, "Is my child gay?" there is no simple answer. A young person's sexual preference often emerges gradually. She may struggle over time to understand her complex feelings. Some research shows that young people confused by same-sex attraction take a break from considering the subject at all, then approach the subject again at a later point. Talking with a supportive third party, such as a therapist, can help you and your daughter understand her feelings and deal with your own.

"This boy I went out with kept talking about sex. I told him I was not like his other girlfriends and that I was holding on to my virginity. Not only do I not want to get diseases, pregnant, or a broken heart—I respect my body, and when you have sex, it's like giving yourself away. He said we could use condoms and talked about abortion, and I am not used to boys talking about that stuff to me. I felt uncomfortable because I'm young and we did go to

third base. It made me feel like a slut. I guess I did it because I didn't want to ruin anything. I wish I had spoken up because now I feel kind of ashamed. But I am glad I said no to going all the way. I still say sex can wait. If you really respect your body, you will wait until you're married to have sex."

Age 14

Dr. Ponton: This girl has had a disturbing and upsetting date. She felt awful that this boy made it to "third base" but was glad she refused to "go all the way." Admittedly, this is not an easy area to discuss, but girls often tell me they want to share parts of their experiences with their parents. You may wonder if the terms this girl uses mean what they did when you were young. Checking with my teen friends, *first base* is kissing, *second base* is sexual touching that occurs above the waist, and *third base* is sexual touching below the waist. Third base may or may not include oral sex. It does not include vaginal intercourse, which is most often described as *going all the way* or *a home run.*

If your daughter brings up her experiences, be a good listener and try not to turn into the "sex police." Reminding her of the risks and that she has choices is one thing; lecturing her about something she already feels bad about is another. If your daughter went further than she was comfortable with because, like this girl, she "didn't want to ruin anything," find out what consequences she feared. Did she think the boy would break up with her if she didn't? Did she think stopping him would disrupt the already established sequence of their sexual behavior? Make sure your daughter understands that she always has the right to say "no" to sexual activity, no matter what has gone on before, and that she knows what she can say to a boy when she's in this situation.

"How do I deal with a breakup?"
"After going out with a guy for a year and a half, he dumped me. He said it was because we grew apart, but I'm almost positive it was because this other girl was all over him. Music is important to me, so I wrote a lot of songs to help deal with it, but it's been five months since the breakup and I still hurt. Sometimes I think the pain won't go away."

Age 15

Dr. Ponton: Breakups are difficult at any age. Through songwriting, this girl has developed a strategy that has helped her deal with her experience. Creative activities of all types—journaling, acting, writing poetry, or painting—are helpful not only for developing skills but also for processing and letting painful feelings out. Talking to friends and parents is another strategy. If your daughter is still hurting months after the breakup, let her know it is not unusual to still be in pain. Clearly, this girl is working toward understanding her feelings and accepting a situation she may not be able to change.

"The media think that kids are sex-crazed."

"People who make TV shows and movies make it seem like it is okay for kids to have sex because of their hormones. When the media show young people having sex, the kids watching it think, 'It's okay, because the people on TV did it. Besides, it's just our raging hormones and we're going through changes, so it's okay to act like this.'"
Age 13

Dr. Ponton: This girl is an excellent critic, recognizing that some kids justify their behavior by blaming it on raging hormones and media portrayals of teen life. Yet her cynicism belies that she knows these are poor excuses for risky and complex behavior. Overly simplistic explanations like "raging hormones" don't fool many daughters. Our girls want and need conversations about the complexities of teenage sexual behavior.

If your daughter shares feelings such as these, use her healthy skepticism and strong views to engage her in a conversation about the media. How do they get away with portraying teenage sex simplistically? Why are images of teenagers' bodies used to sell so many products? If she wants to take an activist stance, encourage her to write marketers and network executives about their portrayals of teens. Even if she does not go that far, your conversation has shown her that her opinion is valid and has merit.

YOUR ROLE

Start early. Discussions about relationships and sex need to start by the time your daughter is age six. Don't go into details she's not ready to handle. If she asks a specific question, respond and ask, "Does that answer your question?" Topics will shift as she ages.

Think quantity <u>and</u> quality. One talk isn't enough. You'll need many conversations in which you both talk and listen, sharing morals and values. Use examples from the media and other daily experiences as starters for brief, but important, talks.

Teach her that sex has emotional repercussions. Young people often know the mechanics of sex but don't understand its emotional impact. One of your biggest obstacles is to overcome the attitude that sex is no big deal.

Foster openness. Start saying the magic words, "You can ask me anything," when your daughter is young. Keep that message coming as she grows up—even when the questions get tougher.

Teach her that her body has boundaries. Let her know at a young age that she's the *only* person who can decide how she is touched.

Friends first, boyfriends later. Don't push her into having a boyfriend. Encourage friendships with boys when she's young so that she doesn't build up a mystique about the opposite sex.

Teach her to recognize her inner warning signals. Encourage her to listen to her intuition and feelings and to use her voice. If a boy makes her feel uncomfortable—or if she finds herself afraid to speak up about what she does or doesn't want—that's a red flag.

Educate yourself. Be knowledgeable about sexual issues. You are your daughter's best ally.

Being True to Herself

by Virginia Beane Rutter, M.S.

"I've never taken a stand on anything. Whatever my friends say, whether I agree with them or not, I always say yes. Maybe I will learn to take a stand for myself when I get older."

Age 11

In adolescence, girls face choices and risks that challenge them to develop a strong psychological core. During these years, your daughter will struggle as never before with forming her identity and knowing herself. She will analyze her every tear, word, and thought, every detail of her body and appearance. She will question what she wants to eat; what she thinks about drugs, alcohol, and politics; and what moves her spiritually. Along with her own ruthless self-examination, she will question all that and more in her parents and friends.

This analysis is part of your daughter's search for her own integrity, of learning to make moral decisions that define who she is. Yet with the opinions of family, parents, and peers ringing in her ears, she may find it difficult to hear the quiet voice at her own center that encourages her to think for herself, speak her mind, make judgments and decisions, and choose actions that are true to her.

As her peer group becomes increasingly important to her,

your daughter may lose herself at times, as has the young girl whose letter opens this chapter. This girl is doing what her friends say, although she does not know whether she even trusts those friends to make good decisions for themselves, much less for her. She expresses a weakly voiced hope that she'll develop a mind of her own sometime. But she is on shaky ground. Although she seems to have a vague sense of her own beliefs, she never asserts herself. Unless someone intervenes to help her begin to stand up for herself, she will remain forlorn.

Forming a Strong Mind

We parents are our daughters' first teachers. Mothers are important role models, helping their daughters develop a core self. Mom, as your daughter sees you and other adult women behave in strong, self-respecting ways, she will take those lessons to heart. Later those lessons will resonate as part of her "inner voice," the force that guides her to know how to handle difficult decisions.

Dad, you play an equally crucial role, not only by supporting your daughter as she defines herself and acts on her beliefs but also by showing her that you respect her mother and other women you know. Parents, your daughter watches both of you as she hones her critical skills and forms her values. But at this stage of her life, you gradually must give her more and more responsibility for thinking through problems and making her own decisions.

Having a strong sense of right and wrong is crucial for your daughter's moral and ethical development. As her parents, you instill that conscience in her. But as she begins to think for herself, she also begins to evaluate her parents' and family's judgments

"I think some of the people in my family are racist, and I find it disturbing that they are teaching children bad things. They need to show us what is right. I stand up for what I believe, and I think I always will."

Age 13

about right and wrong. She sees whether or not you act on the beliefs you espouse, and she is acutely sensitive to the discrepancies between what you say and what you do. If she sees or hears you operating with double standards, she may be quick to point out your deceit. Be honest with your daughter about your own behavior, and own up to your inconsistencies.

Your daughter is never too young to begin grappling with ethical issues. If she is faced with a moral dilemma in fifth grade when she sees a classmate cheating on a test, listen to her discomfort or outrage and help her sort out her options. Should she tell the teacher? What are the ramifications if she does or doesn't? What is her responsibility to her class, to the community, and to herself? At the dinner table or when driving her to after-school activities, start discussions about politics, environmental issues, and other social concerns. This kind of dialogue sharpens her thinking skills and expands her awareness of larger issues past the often narrow world of teen concerns. Express your values, but do not use your discussions as a platform for expressing your own views. Rather, seek to elicit her reactions. You'll be helping her practice defining herself in matters of importance, and your respect for her opinions will strengthen your relationship.

Acknowledging Her Feelings

Learning to think for herself is not enough. For your daughter to have emotional authenticity and integrity, she also has to acknowledge all of her feelings, not just the socially acceptable ones. This is especially important for girls because they have traditionally been taught to be pleasing, sweet, and nice. She will be going against this stereotype if she develops a strong character and speaks up for herself during adolescence. Encourage your daughter to be emotionally real with herself and others. This means that when, as a preteen, she begins to withdraw or be angry with you, you will understand her need to separate from you and find her own individual views. Your daughter needs your support in order to stand up for what she believes in. She needs to know that it

"I'm a bold person and I say what I think. Once, my principal was making changes to the school that the kids didn't like. I started a petition and lots of people signed. It didn't change her mind, but it showed her what we really thought. Speaking out may get you in trouble sometimes, but you should do it when it's important."
Age 12

is all right to cause a fuss, make others unhappy with her, or create a conflict if she is taking a stand for her own moral values.

Model the value of making room for negative feelings by sharing your painful feelings with your daughter in appropriate ways. In the daily routine of life, if you are upset, angry, or sad, let her know without taking it out on her. If a family member dies, or if you are going through a divorce or other crisis, mourn your loss and give her the opportunity to express herself in her own way. Talk about her feelings and yours, and resolve conflicts with her in healthy ways that reconnect you after a blowup. Working through the shadowy side of life is just as important as celebrating the productive, happy side.

Being Herself *and* Belonging

One of the biggest conflicts for an adolescent is that she wants desperately to be accepted, to belong to a group. This means that there is often an acute conflict between a girl's individual wishes

and her desire to concede to everything her peers believe, think, and
want her to do in order to join the
club. At the same time, she is also
learning from her peers in healthy
ways. Walking the fine line between
her individuality and relating to her
friends may make your daughter
anxious. Teenagers can be cruel

*"Sometimes I won't speak my mind
because I know this one girl will
think I'm dumb. She won't say it
out loud, but I can see it in her
actions when she gives me this look
like I'm so stupid. Then she will
turn to her friend and give her one
of 'those looks' about me."*
Age 15

and ostracize those who do not go along with the group. It
takes a strong sense of self for your daughter to dare to be different. But she may find her own ground if she is brave enough to
endure some social disapproval for not going along with unhealthy
peer behavior.

The girl in our introductory letter never speaks up, and hence
she is at risk not only for being bullied but also for growing up to
be a woman who does not know who she is. She needs a parent or
mentor to intervene and help her learn to differentiate her feelings
and thoughts, and then she needs to have the courage to express
those hard-won convictions to her friends. If you notice your
daughter going along with her crowd, evaluate the situation discreetly from a distance. Ask her how she feels about always doing
what her friends want her to do. Talk to her in a matter-of-fact, concerned way without trying to impose your views on her. If she is
open to your input, offer gentle suggestions as to how she might
change her behavior. Say, for example, "Next time, why don't you
say, 'Last time we saw the movie *you* wanted to see. This time I'd
really like to choose.'" But if she is too resistant to working it
through with you, speak to a trusted friend or professional about
how you can support your daughter in becoming more empowered.

Teaching Her to Hear Her Inner Voice

As active and busy as her life may be, your daughter also needs
solitude for her emotional and mental well-being. When she is
alone she will tap into her own wellspring and renew herself, and
her creativity will come bubbling up. Give her permission to
explore her rich inner life; her self-esteem is built on that foundation. The more self-reflection she fosters, the more she will know
herself and be true to herself when it comes to working toward
her own goals. If she keeps a journal to write down her feelings,
ideas, and fantasies, tell her to keep it to herself until (if and when)
she is ready to share her ideas or test them out with you, her
teachers, or her friends. She can also nurture and strengthen herself by paying attention to her dreams and fantasies and by reading good books with female heroines. If she is grounded in her
own thoughts, feelings, and imagination, she will be less susceptible to destructive peer pressure.

Time alone, when it has a purpose, can become sacred.
Whether she retreats to her room or to a favorite spot, she can feel
her own wholeness. Your daughter may find a spot in nature—a
creek, a park, or a mountain—where she goes to sit and collect
herself. Once she has learned this skill, she will be able to renew
herself whenever she feels depleted. With self-reflection and self-
nurturing, a girl can discover what gives her life meaning.

Guiding Her Spirit

Your daughter's spirit is the life energy that moves through her.
It is an expression of her individuality. Her spirituality is her connection to something beyond herself. Both spiritedness and
spirituality sustain a girl and contribute to her strong character
and ability to make moral decisions.

"My religion has helped me make many important decisions, such as not smoking, drinking, dressing immodestly, watching R-rated movies, or dating until I'm 16 years old. These are special decisions that will continue to help me as I grow into a teenager. Following my religious beliefs has helped me feel safe and more confident about dealing with situations that might go against my standards."
Age 12

In her preteen and teenage years, you will see your daughter experience a spiritual awakening. As she strives to make sense of the world, her religious faith may help her find her way. Fostering spirituality in your daughter can strengthen and sustain her throughout her life. If your religious tradition includes the Jewish bat mitzvah or Christian confirmation, the ceremony will also mark an ending to middle school and the threshold to high school.

This is also a time in your daughter's life when she will start to examine and question the spiritual faith her family or friends share. Teenagers question, resist, and test their faiths, just as they question everything else they encounter. It is a natural part of the developmental process that she must go through in order to form her own identity, separate from yours.

If she struggles with some of your beliefs, try not to dismiss her actions as a rebellion against you—they are an exploration of her heart. What most of us want is for our daughters to have a faith that supports and sustains them. I recommend embracing your daughter's exploration. It may be a supreme test of your parenting, because it

"I hardly ever go to church, but my beliefs in God and religion are very strong. Technically, I'm Lutheran, but I don't think all my beliefs correspond with the Lutheran ones. I believe God is always there, and no matter how bad something is, it could have been worse if God wasn't there with you. Usually I rely on instinct to make choices, but again, I believe God influences my instinct."
age 13

can feel threatening to have her contradict you on such heartfelt topics. But this process of questioning, examining, and testing religious principles and practices for herself is the only way she can make the beliefs her own. In many cases she will move through this process and come back to your faith in the end. You may be pleasantly surprised at the stimulating relationship you can develop discussing spiritual issues.

Don't let fear that your daughter may choose a faith other than your own undermine your love for her. If you give in to that fear, you will squelch her expression and developing individuality. It can be a privilege to watch her mind and spirit unfold. In your conversations, explain your own beliefs but do not insist that she agree with you. In the long run, talking about her doubts and looking for answers can actually strengthen her spiritual life. If you respond thoughtfully as your daughter faces these crossroads and crises, you will help her grow into a woman who is able to meet life's events and obstacles with faith and compassion.

Virginia Beane Rutter is a mother, teacher, and author of **Celebrating Girls: Nurturing and Empowering Our Daughters** *and* **Embracing Persephone: How To Be the Mother You Want for the Daughter You Cherish.** *She is a practicing marriage and family therapist and certified Jungian analyst, specializing in feminine psychology.*

LISTENING IN

Ms. Beane Rutter responds to girls' concerns about standing their ground, making tough decisions, and defining their spirituality.

"I have a hard time speaking my mind."

"There's a boy in my class whose cheeks are naturally flushed pink. Because of that, the other boys call him 'girl.' They won't let him stand in the boys' line. They say he wears a bra and women's underwear. I want to help him, but then the boys would start teasing me. I don't know what to do."
Age 11

Ms. Beane Rutter: One of the most common moral dilemmas that your daughter faces as a preteen will occur when she sees one person in a group being singled out to be scapegoated. The person targeted usually has a characteristic that makes him or her different. The girl who wrote this letter feels sorry for the boy who has become the butt of jokes made by boys who are trying to shore up their own "masculinity" by putting him down. But she wonders how to help this boy without bringing the bullies' wrath down on herself. She has the first part of the equation: she knows her own values.

If your daughter finds herself in this situation and she tells you about it (or you are lucky enough to pick up on it), praise her for her moral stance and sympathize with her plight. Offer some suggestions. For example, she might quietly befriend the boy and talk to him about his feelings. Or, with your assistance, perhaps she could enlist the help of her teacher. If the teacher handles the situation in a capable, fair way, not only will the entire class learn a lesson but your daughter will win a moral victory.

"I want to become a vegetarian because I feel eating animals is cruel. My dad and my stepmom think that's weird and continue to make me eat meat against my will. I'm 13! Aren't I old enough to make this choice myself?"
Age 13

Ms. Beane Rutter: Many girls decide to become vegetarian in their teens, either out of sympathy for animals or because of ecological concerns. The young teenager who wrote this letter is asserting strong feelings. Her parents are not respecting her choice or her right to control her own body in a healthy way. Their dismissive attitude may undermine her confidence in making other choices. By calling their daughter's food preference weird instead of taking up the issue of health, her parents threaten to turn her exploration into a power struggle that could lead to disturbances around food issues as she grows older.

It is unwise to force your daughter to eat anything against her will. Rather, offer her healthy choices and discuss the health consequences of certain diets— for example, the importance of getting enough protein on a vegetarian diet. Seek connection with your daughter over highly charged issues like this one. Any power struggle with her at this stage may alienate her just when you need a solid relationship.

"I feel strong when I say how I really feel."

"Once I took a stand in front of my class about a little boy from Cuba whose mother died trying to bring him to the United States. I felt a little alone because nobody agreed with me, but a month later the topic came up again and some people did take my side. Even though it wasn't many people, I still felt great."
Age 10

Ms. Beane Rutter: Speaking out makes a girl feel strong. This girl had the courage and sense of self to take a risk that could have alienated her from her classmates. Instead, she reaped the rewards of being true to herself by seeing some of her peers come around to her point of view.

If your daughter brings up current events topics after school or during dinner, ask her questions. Answer the questions she has, and work on finding out her opinions and feelings. Listen with care and ask more questions to help her clarify her thinking and feeling skills. If she finds herself in a situation like this girl's, help her tough out the feeling of standing alone. Our daughters need to be able to endure difficult emotions such as loneliness or sadness for the sake of a higher value. And we have to refrain from trying to protect them from the shadowy aspects of life, lest we prevent them from growing up.

"I don't care what people have to say about my views. I have strong opinions. I don't expect people to understand me sometimes, just as I don't expect to understand other people at times. If I feel someone doesn't understand my view, I will explain it better, until they understand where I am coming from. No one has to agree; they just have to realize that there are other choices and opinions in life."
Age 14

Ms. Beane Rutter: This young woman is developing good judgment about herself and others. She is able to have her own opinions and respect those of others—a very mature point of view. If she is reflecting her parents' teaching, they have done a good job! Of course, she will be tested when she is challenged to act on her views in the face of others' disapproval. How will she decide what to do and still respect others' differences?

As a parent, you do your best job if you show tolerance in your attitudes. You want your daughter to be able to come to you if she has a difficult decision to make. You want her to know that you will listen with an open mind, help her negotiate the problem, and make her own decision.

"When I have a hard decision to make, I don't do it alone."
"When I have to make a difficult decision, I think about my mom and dad. If I ever did anything really bad, I would feel sorry for them. People would think they raised me wrong when they didn't. My mom and dad are stricter than a lot of parents, though, so sometimes I regret their influence."
Age 13

Ms. Beane Rutter: Teenagers care what their parents think of them, and that's good. It is a sign of devotion and healthy attachment that a girl cares about her parents' feelings. But I worry that this young woman is a little *too* concerned about not hurting her parents, and that she will not be able to develop her own sense of judgment of right and wrong. She is following her parents' rules because of how others would judge her mother and father if she did not. She loves her parents and wants to protect their reputation. But instead, she needs to take their moral teachings and make them her own. Also, she chafes at her parents' strictness, which could result in her acting out against their rules.

Parents who are too rigid and

those who are too permissive both let their daughters down. Healthy, strong girls have parents who are loving and set fair limits on age-appropriate behavior. If your 13-year-old daughter says you are being too strict, sit down with her and ask what she means. Be open to changing your views if she is willing to compromise and respect your role as a parent. If you negotiate so that she can join her peers in a healthy way, she can respect your wishes *and* test her mettle in her world.

"My older brother is 18 years old and really cool. He doesn't do drugs, and he has an awesome group of friends, even though you wouldn't call him 'popular.' He has taught me there are some things you don't need to have in order to be cool and have great friends. He doesn't know he influences me, but he does. I am glad I have such a weird but cool brother."
Age 14

Ms. Beane Rutter: Older siblings and cousins have a big influence on adolescent girls. This girl admires her brother for being different from the crowd and holding his own. He has not gone the route of drug experimentation in high school,

and he has good friends. This girl's appreciation for her older brother may reduce her anxiety about being accepted in high school. With him as a model, she will be more confident that she, too, can forge her individual path and still have friends.

It is easier for a girl to learn by example from family members who are closer to her own age than from her parents' experience. But hearing your stories of having lived through similar ordeals does reassure her that she, too, will master such situations. If your daughter's older sibling, however, had traumas in high school, either academically or socially, you will need to prepare her for a different experience. Tell her she has every chance of succeeding on her own merit, even though her older brother or sister had difficulties.

"Spirituality guides my life."
"There are many different religions out there. I'm Protestant, but I still respect other people's feelings and religions. Religion should represent your deepest beliefs, and if you do not agree with the beliefs of your church, then there is a problem! I believe that people should have the right to believe in whatever they

wish, and not just because it was taught in their family."
Age 13

Ms. Beane Rutter: This mature 13-year-old has an open attitude toward religious beliefs. I believe that as parents, we should share our spiritual traditions with our daughters, but if they show an interest in other philosophies, we should support their search for what is meaningful to them. During adolescence, a time of change and intense peer interaction, a Catholic girl might go to Jewish synagogue for services with her friend, or an Episcopalian girl might attend a teaching at the ashram that her boyfriend's family goes to. During this time of exploration, the only sacred energy that sustains a girl is that which touches her personally in a deep way. To claim her faith as her own, she needs to search, question, and find answers for herself.

"I believe God is inside me. He is in my mind and heart, so when I get the instinct that something is wrong and that I shouldn't do it, I figure it is Him telling me that."
Age 14

Ms. Beane Rutter: This girl has a firm faith and feels strongly that
God guides her life. She relates her instincts and her personal conscience to her relationship with God, and that gives her a deep sense of trust in herself and in her own judgments and decisions. When the going is tough, she listens to this strong inner voice.

Your daughter's spiritual conviction can buoy her through the storms of adolescence. As her friends pull her this way and that, and you, her parents, try to help her steer a steady course, she can turn inward to the rock of her belief. As she encounters personal disappointment, hurt, envy, failure, or success, she will then have the sense that something larger than herself is holding her. Support your daughter's affiliation with the spirit; her belief in the divine order of the universe will give her a meaningful context for her life.

"I pray to God to help me get through things, make things happen, or solve things that are really important to me. Sometimes it seems like my prayers are answered, but sometimes it just seems like no one is actually up there. But I pray anyway because it feels like there's someone to

talk to and it's good to think and get stuff out."
Age 14

Ms. Beane Rutter: While struggling with questions of faith, this girl is forming her core identity. She is finding out that prayer itself makes her feel better, whether or not she feels her prayers are answered. She is developing an attitude of the sacred. Whether she is affiliated with a church, synagogue, mosque, or Buddhist temple, it is valuable if your daughter has a sense of power beyond herself. Knowing her own soul and feeling grace within and thanksgiving for her life will sustain her during difficult times.

"I don't agree with my parents about religion."

My dad and I disagree on religion and feminism. He thinks I'm a feminist and that the Bible says I'm wrong. But I don't think I am. I just have different views."
Age 12

Ms. Beane Rutter: Our daughters should not have to choose between their relationships with us and their own identities. It would be better if this father could be more tolerant of his daughter's views and encourage her to think for

herself. Otherwise he risks alienating her or interfering with her ability to trust her own thoughts, feelings, and decisions. She may think she has to choose between siding with him out of respect or pursuing her independent thinking. If her father could begin a conversation by saying, "Honey, this is my understanding of the Bible, but I'd like to hear what you are thinking, studying, and feeling," our letter writer would be able to respect his views and her own.

As parents, we have to expand our relationship wide enough to include our own identities and our daughters'. If this father pushes his daughter too far, she may reject the Bible altogether, but if he lets her discover her own way, he may find that she comes back to his faith with renewed vigor after she has explored other paths.

"I am Christian, but my parents are not. We fight about it a lot. They don't let me go to church and they don't like it when I talk about what I believe. Sometimes it hurts because I don't have anybody to talk to about the things that are most important to me, and I feel like my parents don't understand me. My parents are not very strict, and

sometimes when I make a decision I think is right, such as not going to parties with older kids, they don't understand why. It's very hard to be different from my parents, but I will never give up my faith for anyone."
Age 13

Ms. Beane Rutter: It may be that this girl's religion provides her with rules and guidance for her behavior that her parents are not giving. She seems to be suffering from their lack of setting limits and from not being able to share herself with them. In trying to communicate with them about her faith, she is asking them to understand her.

Strive to be tolerant and open, be curious about your daughter's interests, and learn from her about them. With some self-reflection and an awareness of who she is, you will be able to figure out what she sees in a religious or community group. You may determine that she is exploring the world and its possibilities or that she's missing something from you.

YOUR ROLE

Value relationship over control. To have influence over your daughter, you must gradually give up managing every aspect of her life. This will help her become responsible for her choices.

Encourage her to trust herself. Advise your daughter to listen to her inner voice, her feminine intuition, or her hunches. Teach her that these impulses come from deep within and can often inform her in ways that reason cannot.

Don't hold back. Sharing stories of your own moral dilemmas shows your daughter that you trust her. Just do not expect that she will solve a problem in the same way you did.

Expand her mind. Make sure your daughter reads literature that presents moral and spiritual dilemmas solved in a variety of ways. She will learn from stories of young people who were faced with decisions and guided by good values.

Value her heritage. Whatever your roots, teach your daughter to appreciate her heritage through family stories or cultural celebrations. This knowledge will make her feel grounded and strong and help her better understand herself.

Be open to her spiritual exploration. Support your daughter in her quest for her spirituality. No matter what faith she is raised in, if she is deeply spiritual she is likely to question her religion and investigate other faiths at some time. It is wise to let her go to different religious institutions with friends and explore other traditions so that she can come to her own inner faith.

Reaching for the Stars

by Roni Cohen-Sandler, Ph.D.

"I am beginning to realize what actually goes on in the world. When my parents watch the news, I always hear about wars, and it upsets me that people are fighting. I am Jewish and my religion's home country is Israel. The Israelis are in a war with the Palestinians, and I want that war to stop. When I grow up, I am going to help solve people's conflicts and make peace. I am beginning to work for that goal. I am in a conflict-resolution program at school, and I help students solve conflicts in a peaceful manner. I might be young, but I can help make the world go round."

Age 9

By the end of the elementary school years, many girls begin to look beyond the boundaries of their present individual worlds—family, friends, and school—to envision new possibilities for themselves and, sometimes, even for the entire universe. During this stage, great discoveries and big dreams help your daughter shape her life. Her ambitions direct her energies, motivate her to apply herself in school or activities, and influence decisions whose effects are lifelong. She may aspire to achieve distinction in writing, science, acting, or sports. She may want to win awards. She may aim for glory or prestige. In fact, increasingly aware of an entire future awaiting her, your daughter's hopes may be virtually limitless. Like many girls her age, she may even ponder how she can change the world. Many factors make these dreams possible.

As her cognitive abilities mature, your daughter's perspective expands. She begins to see the bigger picture—the forest as well as the trees. Her improved reading skills enable her to learn more sophisticated material in greater depth. As she forms concepts, analyzing and reflecting on her experiences, she is able to take her intellectual curiosity to the next level. She may search out deeper meanings within her experiences, asking, "Why is this important to me?" and "What really matters in this world?" She will empathize more with others, and that will ignite her compassion and altruism.

As the girl in our introductory letter demonstrates, even young girls may dream of taking on global problems. That is partly because today's technology exposes our daughters far sooner and more powerfully to pressing social issues. Girls do not just hear about past wars or remote hardships; they witness graphic portrayals of tragedies and injustices broadcast into their own homes. Although some girls may become anxious and overwhelmed by these indelible images, many channel their dismay into aspirations that become guiding forces in their lives. This young girl is confident she can right the wrongs she perceives and bring peace to the world, in part because she has been able to develop real-life strategies that put her values to work. She has actually seen her conflict-resolution efforts succeed at school.

As your own daughter expresses such grand plans, you may witness a new kind of seriousness and determination in her demeanor. Her youthful idealism can be motivating—and often infectious. But what should you do if her dreams seem unrealistic and you fear she is headed for disappointment? More importantly, how can you empower your daughter so that, like our letter writer, she is bursting to fulfill her dreams?

Benefit from Her Energy

To your daughter, life's possibilities can appear infinite. Her curiosity and energy may seem boundless to you. Like a sponge, she soaks up whatever ideas intrigue her. She is delighted by the fresh avenues she can explore and goals she can achieve. She can be so impressionable that an enthusiastic individual, special moment, or successful experience may kindle brand-new passions. For example, after hearing the speech of a well-known, charismatic activist, my teen-age daughter suddenly developed a zest for the political process. That is why it is important to give your daughter as many enriching experiences as possible and to expose her to experts in diverse fields.

> *"My goal is to go to Princeton University and work for NASA as a rocket engineer. I have wanted to do this for a long time."*
> age 14

As she pursues her interests, your daughter gains much in the process. Sorting through her own experiences and preferences gives her crucial information about herself. She discovers that some activities are merely temporary diversions and that there are others in which she wants to excel. She learns which causes she believes in with all her heart. You probably have strong opinions about these issues, too, and your ideas have been shaped by your own triumphs and disappointments. But give your daughter a chance to draw her own conclusions and make her own choices. The more she is encouraged to use her genuine feelings as her guide, the better she will come to know and trust herself. The processes of refining her goals and redefining herself go hand in hand.

Believe in Her Dreams

Many parents worry that if they are not Olympic athletes, musical maestros, or past leaders of some high school team, they cannot possibly help their daughter fulfill her goals. Fortunately, this is far from true. Regardless of our backgrounds, the greatest gift we can give our girls is simple: taking our daughters seriously and believing in their dreams. Nothing can be more empowering or motivating than conveying the message to your daughter, "I believe in you." And your support should not be confined merely to your words. Consider what the everyday tasks you do for your daughter communicate about your attitude. Do you drive her cheerfully to her practices, lessons, and games and pick her up on time? Do you keep track of her schedule and attend her events? What does your daughter hear you say about her dreams as you speak with others?

We also inspire our daughters indirectly, not through what we say or do about their goals but in how we conduct our own lives. That is why we need to be scrupulously self-aware. How do we handle being harried or feeling overwhelmed by responsibilities? How do we cope with the sting of disappointment or failure? How and when do we adjust our personal goals? It may be daunting to consider the many daily opportunities you have to model stamina, flexibility, persistence, and determination. But when you demonstrate these desirable qualities, be assured that your daughter is watching closely and appreciatively.

Your daughter needs practical guidance as well. She needs you to connect what she is doing now—her education, practice, and training—with her future goals. No matter how motivated she is, she has to translate her dreams into a viable course of action. This enables her to develop what David Stevenson and

Barbara Schneider, authors of the book *The Ambitious Generation,* describe as "aligned ambitions"—ambitions combined with clear and realistic life plans for reaching them. Teenagers who do not see how their dreams can actually become reality tend to become "drifting dreamers." Even if your daughter's goals have seemingly low odds for success, assess whether her plans are consistent with those goals and whether they are specific enough. Such preparation is crucial to fulfilling all dreams.

Fuel Her Passion for a Cause

Girls are motivated to achieve goals not just for themselves but also to correct inequities and make the world a better, fairer place. Historically, many of our social reforms were, in fact, sparked by individuals who saw injustices and worked to correct them.

When your daughter is impassioned by a cause, you may have mixed feelings. You may find her concerns admirable yet want to protect her from the trials that pioneers often experience as they make groundbreaking strides. If your daughter's beliefs make her stand out from the crowd in any way, or if there is resistance to the changes she advocates, she will probably not have an easy time of it during adolescence. Several girls I know fought to be included on traditionally all-boy sports teams, only to find the strain of being tormented intolerable once they made the team. Should your daughter find herself in this position, your sensitivity will be invaluable. You support her beliefs, but probably not at the cost of her well-being. She might need you to give her permission to say, "I've had enough."

> *"One of my goals in life is to play pro baseball. I really love the game, and I don't think it's fair that they don't let women in the professional leagues. I want to be the first woman to play in the major leagues."*
> Age 11

The Voice of Support or the Voice of Reason?

In spite of their bravado, girls usually look to adults for validation and confirmation. Thus, when our daughters entrust us with their deep-seated dreams, they feel vulnerable and may become highly attuned to even the subtlest of reactions. They want to know whether we think their goals are foolish or really can be achieved.

> *"My aspiration is to be an author, and my mother encourages me a lot. She is a writer and has published two books. I'm so proud of her. Whenever I win awards for my writing, she says she knew I would all along."*
> Age 13

Your daughter is counting on you to understand her dreams. In order to do so, focus on what these dreams mean to her rather than to you. This may be more easily said than done; her dreams may be vastly different from your plans for her. Perhaps it is difficult to relate to her passions. You may be drawn to technology, while she may live to create art. Such differences may make you uneasy. Also, since supporting your daughter in her aspirations requires you to invest time, emotional energy, and financial resources, you will probably develop your own hopes and dreams for her. This is normal, but remember that those are not *her* dreams.

Keep in mind that what often appeals to preteen or teenage girls may be completely undesirable to their parents, for a variety of valid reasons. Perhaps you believe your daughter is being impractical or has unrealistic expectations. In fact, you may be correct that she does not understand what her goals will truly require of her in the long run. As parents, we like to think that we know best—and that we know our daughters best. At

> *"My parents always criticize me about my dreams and tell me to get my head out of the clouds. I feel like my heart is being stabbed every time I talk about who I want to be and they don't listen."*
> Age 14

times, we may believe we have more control over our children's destiny than we actually do. But if we try to stop our daughters from following their dreams, not only is it unlikely they will appreciate our advice, but they also may become resentful or rebellious.

Your daughter's age is a key factor in deciding whether you should offer unconditional support or be the voice of reason. When she is relatively young, you have fewer worries about being pragmatic. A ten-year-old need not be concerned with the obstacles to becoming a star in her chosen field or to obtaining a well-paying job to support herself. As she matures and is faced with making life-shaping decisions, help her achieve a healthy balance in her approach. Even though you should not rule out any possibilities, give her the freedom to take appropriate risks and even stumble. When you listen attentively to your daughter's dreams and give her the chance to explore her passions, you are endorsing her wholeheartedly. In contrast, negative comments or dismissive remarks are like pinpricks, instantly deflating her confidence along with her lofty aspirations.

Deal with Disappointment

Along with dreams comes potential disappointment. When your daughter dares to hope, there is always a chance that those hopes might be dashed. For a variety of reasons, even your daughter's best efforts and your most enthusiastic support may not enable her to achieve her goals. She may not be chosen for that coveted leadership position she craves. The recognition she thinks she deserves may elude her. She may respond by being blasé, sad, furious, or vengeful. She might conclude she is not as talented as she had thought. She may redouble her efforts to succeed or impulsively quit the activity altogether.

These dilemmas are even more frustrating when they are caused by factors outside her control. Your daughter may get sick or experience terrible stress at a time when it means everything for her to be in top form. Or her failure may be the result of simple misfortune: a cancellation because of bad weather or other twist of fate. In some cases, the situation may be truly unfair; your daughter clearly may not be afforded the same advantages as a rival. It would be wise to take the position that neither you nor she can ever control all the factors determining her success.

You cannot assure your daughter that life will be fair, but you can promise to support her in handling whatever does happen. Try to understand and empathize with her feelings in ways that insure she does not feel dismissed. You may want to reflect, "I can see how disappointed you are," or "You seem confused about what you want to do now," rather than saying, "Well, you knew this was possible!" or "What's the big deal? You'll have other chances."

If her goals are too ambitious, influence her to make appropriate adjustments as she experiences frustration and setbacks. She may come to see that her ultimate goal has become less important to her than it once was. Perhaps she will discover that being a superstar is not possible—or not all she had anticipated. Your gift may be to help her shift her thinking, to value her efforts, and to appreciate what she has learned along the way.

Her Dreams, Your Faults

During the preteen and teenage years, many girls develop goals that go beyond the tangible. Besides identifying particular achievements, they may dream of future lives enriched by grand values and lofty principles. Your daughter may be introspective about her personal qualities, hoping to become a better individual through hard work, kindness, or loyalty. As she considers such virtues, she is apt to observe and even challenge adults who serve as potential role models. You may find your daughter is increasingly critical, determined to poke holes in your beliefs or point out discrepancies in your behavior.

Although it is easy to feel defensive, you might tolerate her inspection better if you understand this behavior as a necessary learning tool. Your daughter is observing you and others closely, both to understand more about herself and to fine-tune the pursuit of her dreams.

Recognizing numerous inequalities in the world, some girls set out to correct injustices and prejudices. Their dreams tell us clearly that these girls are thinking. Instead of merely drifting passively into options, they are actively, consciously pondering possibilities and making deliberate choices. In fact, your daughter is looking for and making her own opportunities. She may be young, but she is thoughtful and contemplative; her new capacity for thinking abstractly and behaving selflessly is shaping her ambitions.

"I would like to run for the office of President of the United States when I'm 35 years old so I can help people from all cultures who live here. My dad was born in a Spanish-speaking country and moved here as an adult. People from other cultures shouldn't be discriminated against in schools, jobs, or anywhere else."
Age 11

Dr. Roni Cohen-Sandler is the author of "I'm Not Mad, I Just Hate You!" *She is a mother and a clinical psychologist specializing in the issues of women and adolescent girls. She is also author of a forthcoming book on mothers, daughters, and teenage social lives.*

LISTENING IN

Making big plans, setting and reaching goals, and sometimes failing . . . Dr. Cohen-Sandler looks at how your daughter can fulfill her dreams and reach her potential—and how you can help.

"I have big dreams and goals."
"I think every girl should have goals. When I first started kung fu six years ago, I had one of the biggest goals: to get my black belt. I did it just last December, and it felt great!"
Age 10

Dr. Cohen-Sandler: Establishing a goal can be a pivotal, positive force in a young girl's life. It can be motivational, offering additional structure and purpose. It can also provide a template she can use to achieve future goals.

When your daughter works toward a goal, she learns how much effort it requires. She will figure out how much time and energy are needed. She will have to choose among other interests and learn that to be successful, she cannot do everything. We can imagine the self-confidence and pride this girl feels in being persistent and successful over the long haul. The joy and sense of accomplishment she expresses after fulfilling her goal is likely to be felt well beyond kung fu.

"Ever since I was eight years old, I have wanted to become a gold-medal Olympic swimmer. A few years ago I was dying to make my camp swim team. When I didn't make it, I was heartbroken. During the fall and winter, I joined a swim team at home and got a lot faster. When I tried out for the camp team the next year, I made it. I realized that if you want to accomplish something, you have to practice a lot. I hope that if I practice a lot, I will make it to the Olympics."
Age 11

Dr. Cohen-Sandler: Our daughters learn a multitude of lessons as they reach for their dreams, and many crucial truths are gained from disappointments. As parents, we probably would prefer to protect our daughters from failure. Who would wish to see a daughter in pain? However, this girl's letter illustrates beautifully what can happen when parents are able to step back and allow their daughters the freedom to experience failure. Despite any self-doubts

she may have had, this girl did not abandon her goal after not making the camp team. Instead, her disappointment fueled her efforts to improve her skills. Accepting responsibility for her situation instead of blaming circumstances outside of her control, she felt able to take charge. She rethought her goals and used new strategies that, combined with determination, brought her closer to her ultimate goal.

If your daughter feels stuck when she hits a barrier, she may need your help to hurdle it. While many girls can identify their dreams, fewer know how to reach them. Your daughter may need help problem solving. You can show her how to break down her goal into smaller, more manageable parts. That way she can plan and carry out the step-by-step actions that will get her where she wants to go.

"It has been my dream to be a professional soccer player since I began playing at age five. This year I was crushed to find out we didn't have enough players to make a team. It made me really sad, but when I found out my little brother's team didn't have an assistant coach,

I volunteered for the job. The season just started and we've already won two games in a row! That makes me very happy. At the last game, one of the players' little sisters told me I was a good coach, and that made me really proud."
Age 14

Dr. Cohen-Sandler: When our daughters journey to the stars, they (and we) never know where detours will take them. As we can see in this letter, sometimes circumstances that initially appear devastating actually can become blessings. A lot depends on a girl's attitude. In this case, our letter writer demonstrated resourcefulness and flexibility in taking lemons and making lemonade. Although she was "really sad" that there was no soccer team for her age group, she took the opportunity to coach younger children. She not only contributed to her community but also honed new skills, saw her efforts pay off, and received meaningful praise. No wonder she is proud!

If your daughter is focused narrowly on only one goal, and particularly if it is unlikely she'll achieve it, she may need your gentle nudging to consider alternatives. In moments of dejection, she may not be able to appreciate your encouraging perspective or take in your heartening stories. Do not take this personally. Only through her own experience will she realize how obstacles occasionally result in new beginnings and mistakes often turn out to be bonuses in the end.

"My parents inspire me."

"My dad and I always go to the bookstore together. He's the type of person who urges me to do what I want, and then he'll be really cool about it."

Age 10

Dr. Cohen-Sandler: Many fathers report that despite their willingness to do so, they are unsure about how to relate to their daughters during the preteen and, especially, the teenage years. As girls mature sexually, dads often withdraw because they get uncomfortable. It is harder to be close, as certain discussions and customary physical activities (horseplay, sitting on laps, and the like) may seem off-limits. When fathers feel uncertain about how to connect, however, they lose invaluable opportunities to shape their daughters' growing sense of self and influence their developing dreams.

As this girl eloquently points out, what our daughters really want is their fathers' attention. Whether Dad takes his daughter to the bookstore, for ice cream, or to the post office, these actions tell her she is important to him. Clearly, many dads want their daughters' company. In choosing to spend time with daughters, fathers send the unmistakable message, "I love you and believe in you." As we have seen in so many letters, girls thrive when their dreams are well supported. No wonder research has shown that a father's involvement contributes to his daughter's sense of her place in the world, her self-esteem, and her later achievement.

"My parents don't understand my dreams."

"My parents say they know me better than anyone, but they don't really know me at all. They don't understand my need to write. I write fiction, and when I write, I'm happier than at any other time. When I'm writing, my parents want me to be doing something else with them, but I really don't want to do it."

Age 13

Dr. Cohen-Sandler: As girls enter the teenage years, their dreams are determined in part by their emotional needs. One girl may choose activities that provide companionship. Another may find appeal in the chance to perform and receive accolades. The girl who wrote this letter revels in the chance to create, stretch her imagination, and perhaps give order to ideas she is struggling with in her own life. When she expresses the joy that writing brings her, she sounds exactly like a true writer.

This girl's parents need to recognize that it is difficult for them to appreciate their daughter's "need to write" because they are not writers themselves. It will mean a great deal if they make an effort to appreciate what writing means to *her*. As the girl indicates in her letter, she experiences her parents' requests to join them in other activities as dismissive of her dreams.

It is understandable that this girl's parents want to spend more time with their daughter. And we all know how easy it is to be bruised by our teenagers' curt refusals of our invitations. But a 13-year-old's desire for solitude is perfectly normal, and writing may give this girl a way to meet

such a need. Whatever your daughter's passion, she will almost always appreciate your inquiries about it. Ask what it feels like to *be* her when she is most engrossed. Ask to see and hear all you can. This girl's parents might bridge the chasm between her and them simply by asking to read her stories. They can encourage her to submit her writing to teen magazines or school literary publications. If this girl is willing to share her writing, her parents will have a wonderful conduit to her thoughts and dreams.

"My dad asked me, 'What do you want to be when you grow up?' When I said I want to be a dancer, he rolled his eyes and said, 'That is not a future!' My mom said my dancing stunk, even though she knew how I felt about dancing."
Age 14

Dr. Cohen-Sandler: As we look into our daughters' futures, it is only natural that we want to see our children being successful. But, as we can see from this letter, girls are terribly injured when parents denigrate their dreams. When we put down their hopes, our daughters feel as if we are disparaging them to their very core. Even if you are convinced your daughter's dream is a long shot, consider the possibility that it could happen. Recently, I read about an 11-year-old boy who began sliding in his socks around the homeless shelter where he lived. His mom responded to his interest and got him involved in figure skating. Many obstacles later, he is an Olympic hopeful with more than two dozen medals. Why not allow your daughter's dreams to soar while you keep one foot solidly on sensible ground?

Your best tactic is to give her basic information about what is required for achievement. Which pathways are available, and what are their advantages and disadvantages? Your daughter needs a plan with realistic, detailed steps to translate her dreams into actual accomplishments. Once she understands her options, you can support her fully as long as she agrees to have a back-up plan. Negotiate a compromise that feels right to both of you. For example, if she hopes to be an opera singer, agree to provide voice and piano lessons as long as she does not fall behind in algebra.

But what about when you truly think your daughter does not have what it takes? How do you walk the fine line between praising falsely and being critical? For starters, focus on your daughter's efforts and enthusiasm. You might say, "I can see how much that means to you," or "You're really working hard at that!" Avoid comments about her limitations that can be construed as put-downs ("You have a long way to go, honey," or "You'd never make it in the real world"). Chances are, your daughter will get the critical feedback she needs about her goals from her teachers, coaches, and mentors.

"Will I ever reach my goal?"

"I have done Irish stepdancing for five years and I've never won anything. I get mad and feel dumb a lot, but I always wanted to win a medal. I know I should keep trying until I reach my goal."
Age 12

Dr. Cohen-Sandler: It is distressing to watch our daughters experience the disappointment that results from unmet goals. Like this girl, some react by putting themselves down because of their failures. They can become angry at the situation, at those involved, at the world, and, especially, at their parents. Some girls also lose hope for the future.

To avoid another letdown after a loss, you may be tempted to dissuade your daughter from continuing to work toward her goal. Yet that would send the message, "Don't try because you might fail." Offer a different perspective: maybe she does not need to try harder but needs to rethink what she hopes to achieve. After some soul-searching, your daughter may find that her original goals are no longer important. For example, there are times when winning is not (and should not be) the only objective. The parents of the girl in this letter should explore why getting a medal in Irish dancing is so crucial to their daughter. She is depriving herself of a sense of accomplishment for her commitment to her dancing and the skills she has developed. These achievements are all worthy of recognition and pride. In many cases, girls may not realize that a trophy earned in a single competition is arbitrary. The real achievements occur during every class and practice session.

"My dream is to win an election. I'm very smart in math, and I ran for school treasurer and lost—to a girl who was failing math! That really depleted my confidence, because she won only because she was popular. The following year I ran for band treasurer. All my friends are in band, and they know I'm a great band student, so I thought I would win. I lost to a girl who was failing band! Again, it was because she was more popular than I was. I would really like to win an election just once."
Age 11

Dr. Cohen-Sandler: "It's not fair!" becomes an anguished refrain when girls fail to attain a prize they believe is rightfully theirs. This girl thinks she earned the recognition and respect of her peers through her achievements and therefore deserves to be elected to office. Although in similar situations your impulse may be to reassure your daughter that "things will turn out all right in the end," it may be more helpful to validate her perception that sometimes they do not. Sometimes, in fact, things are truly unfair. And, as this girl suggests, there is often an irony we may hope to be able to laugh about—someday.

It is also human nature to want something more when we cannot have it. When we fall short of a goal, it often swells in importance and becomes our sole focus.

In fact, it is easy to lose sight of why this goal was important originally. With 20-20 hindsight, you can look back on your own experiences that bear this out. Sharing such stories with your daughter can reassure her. Offering the perspective of time can also be helpful. It is hard for your daughter to recognize that what matters to her peers at age 11 is not, fortunately, what will be important as she gets older. At any age, girls want and need recognition of their talents and achievements. But at times, your daughter might have to be satisfied with knowing that, in her heart of hearts, she was the best candidate for the job, regardless of the outcome.

"I have high hopes for the future."
My goal is to show people that skin color doesn't matter. I'm white, but my best friend is copper-skinned. I'm disgusted when the popular girls at school don't include her. She speaks English and loves the same bands and toys that we do."
Age 9
Dr. Cohen-Sandler: By the preteen and teenage years, girls are studying others carefully to search out similarities and differences. As they try to figure out what makes some of their peers "popular" and others excluded, they become keen detectors of injustice, prejudice, and hypocrisy. This girl expresses her outrage at the blatant inequity she observes and is committed to changing it. Her observations have inspired her to show people a kinder and more inclusive way of thinking.

If you are in a similar situation, you can validate your daughter's values simply by discussing them with her. Help her reach her goal of showing people that skin color does not matter. Explore how she imagines herself in the future, what roles she envisions playing to change people's perceptions, and what it would take to transform these dreams into success. Expose her to stories of others, young and old, who share similar goals. Speak with her about organizations and individuals devoted to civil rights. As she gets older, arrange for her to shadow women who are involved in these activities through Take Our Daughters to Work day. Help her arrange volunteer experiences and, eventually, internships to work for human justice and equity.

"I don't worry about my future, because I am making good choices

right now. But if a person chooses not to do drugs or make other mistakes, she has some control over her future and knows it will be good. I get discouraged when adults say that we are a terrible generation and that we're bound to mess up. I think we're trying hard to make things better, and I think adults should believe in us more."
Age 13

Dr. Cohen-Sandler: This girl's hopefulness is based on her sense that she is in charge of her destiny rather than the pawn of forces outside her control. If your daughter subscribes to this view, she will be empowered to make smarter, more conscious choices instead of behaving passively or unwisely. Research underscores that teen girls who are working toward goals are more likely to delay sexual intercourse and other risky activities.

This girl articulates a complaint not uncommon among young people: that adults can be critical of what they see and fearful of what their children will experience in the future. Eager to stave off deeper problems, we parents can be quick to note the red flags of potential difficulties. Sometimes we overreact and fail to convey confidence that our daughters can work through issues on their own. Take this girl's plea to heart and recognize that this generation of girls is eager not to cause problems but to solve them. Our caring, ambitious, and hopeful daughters cannot wait to fulfill their dreams.

YOUR ROLE

Create inspiration. Encourage your daughter to read biographies of noteworthy individuals, especially women. Point out news stories in which people reach their goals. Take advantage of educational opportunities for girls, particularly in math and the sciences.

Anticipate obstacles. Discuss how novel and untested ideas are usually distrusted and how successful pioneers overcame roadblocks.

Provide mentors. Despite your best efforts, it is unlikely you can give your daughter all the expertise she needs. Mentors can model desirable qualities, inspire her, and nurture her dreams.

Allow her to fail. Failure is a necessary experience. It helps your daughter shift her priorities and adjust her goals.

Search out information. Teach her to use all available resources. She can use the Internet to discover exciting developments in her areas of interest, link up with experts, and find opportunities to observe and participate in others' efforts through local programs.

Accept experimentation. Your daughter's journey through adolescence will likely take its twists and turns. She may try any number of avenues before she finds one that feels right and leads to success.

Use the gift of time. When your daughter insists on pursuing a course of action that makes you uncomfortable, remember that her desires may change over time. Delay big decisions until they are absolutely necessary. Suggest, "Let's give it six months and see where you stand then."

Keep your anxiety in check. Your emotions and relationship with your daughter influence her dreams enormously. If you are unduly hesitant, she may second-guess her goals. But if you believe, she will have the courage to work toward her dreams.

Resource Guide

The following books and organizations can help you guide your daughter through her adolescent years so that she emerges strong and whole on the other side.

Reading Resources

All That She Can Be: Helping Your Daughter Maintain Her Self-Esteem by Carol J. Eagle and Carol Colman (Simon & Schuster Trade, 1994). Sound, comprehensive advice about supporting your daughter as she grows up.

The Ambitious Generation: America's Teenagers, Motivated but Directionless by David Stevenson and Barbara Schneider (Yale University Press, 2000). Advice on how parents can better direct and support young people in their efforts to achieve their goals.

Between Mother and Daughter: A Teenager and Her Mom Share the Secrets of a Strong Relationship by Judy Ford and Amanda Ford (Conari Press, 1999). The real-life experiences of a mother and daughter who have built a lasting relationship.

The Body Project: An Intimate History of American Girls by Joan Jacobs Brumberg (Random House, 1998). An examination of how growing up in a girl's body has changed during the past century and why it is more difficult today than ever before.

The Book of Hopes and Dreams for Girls and Young Women: Notable Women Share Their Experiences and Wisdom, edited by Christine Aulicino and JoAnn Deak (Laurel School, 1999). A collection of inspirational letters written to students by well-known women, including Marian Wright Edelman, Jane Goodall, and Ruth Bader Ginsburg. Colorful artwork and thoughts from girls themselves are mixed in.

Celebrating Girls: Nurturing and Empowering Our Daughters by Virginia Beane Rutter (Conari Press, 1996). A warm-hearted book that reminds parents to be mindful of the moments spent with their daughters and to treasure their gifts.

Cherishing Our Daughters: How Parents Can Raise Girls to

Become Confident Women by Evelyn Bassoff (Dutton Plume, 2000). An insightful exploration of the unique gifts dads and moms bring to parenting. Includes discussions of difficult issues such as setting limits and letting go.

Cliques: Eight Steps to Help Your Child Survive the Social Jungle by Charlene C. Gianetti and Margaret Sagarese (Broadway Books, 2001). Practical advice about disarming bullies and what to do if your child is excluded.

Daughters Newsletter, for Parents of Girls 10 to 16 (Dads and Daughters). An advertising-free newsletter published eight times a year, offering effective parenting and communication techniques to help parents develop strong relationships with their daughters.

The Difference: Discovering the Hidden Ways We Silence Girls— Finding Alternatives That Can Give Them a Voice by Judy Mann (Warner, 1996). Examines how girls are treated differently from boys, as well as how parents can value "the difference" girls bring to our lives and to the world.

Embracing Persephone: How to Be the Mother You Want for the Daughter You Cherish by Virginia Beane Rutter (Conari Press, 2001). A loving exploration of how our daughters find inde-

pendence during their teen years and how that process transforms both them and us.

Failing at Fairness: How Our Schools Cheat Girls by Myra and David Sadker (Simon & Schuster, 1995). A controversial and eye-opening look at inequality in the classroom and ways parents can help.

Fathering: Strengthening Connection with Your Children No Matter Where You Are by Will Glennon (Conari Press, 1995). Explores the essential emotional connection between fathers and children and the courage it takes to father well.

For All Our Daughters: How Mentoring Helps Young Women and Girls Master the Art of Growing Up by Pegine Echevarria (Chandler House, 1998). Practical ideas we can use to teach the girls we mentor about finance, emotional well-being, achievement, health, and taking loving care of themselves.

Games Girls Play by Caroline Silby and Shelley Smith (St. Martin's Press, 2000). Advice that can help any parent support an active girl—with specific exercises for relieving nervousness before sporting events and advice about coaches, parents' roles, and the social and physical problems related to sports.

Girls Seen and Heard: 52 Life Lessons for Our Daughters by Sondra Forsyth (Putnam Publishing Group, 1998). Short essays and inspiring stories about girls and women who learn lessons about personal worth in the world of work.

How Girls Thrive: An Essential Guide for Educators (and Parents) by JoAnn Deak (National Association of Independent Schools, 1998). Strategies to help you build your daughter's confidence.

How to Father a Successful Daughter by Nicky Marone (Fawcett, 1999). Insightful writing from a classroom teacher about girls who lose self-esteem during junior high. Discusses the advantage and responsibility dads have when it comes to encouraging a daughter's achievement and feelings of self-esteem.

How to Mother a Successful Daughter: A Practical Guide to Empowering Girls from Birth to 18 by Nicky Marone (Harmony, 1999). Practical ideas for teaching your daughter "mastery" skills that will encourage her self-confidence and help her achieve.

"I'm Not Mad, I Just Hate You!": A New Understanding of Mother-Daughter Conflict by Roni Cohen-Sandler and Michelle Silver (Viking Penguin, 2000). Suggestions for how to argue less and appreciate each other more. Helps mothers see anger as an emotion they can use to strengthen, not harm, relationships with their daughters.

In a Different Voice: Psychological Theory and Women's Development by Carol Gilligan (Harvard University Press, 1993). A news-making study of the differences between how girls and boys think, with emphasis on making moral decisions.

Keep Talking: A Mother-Daughter Guide to the Pre-Teen Years by Lynda Madison (Andrews McMeel Publishing, 1999). Loving, step-by-step guidance for having meaningful conversations with your daughter through the teen years. A book for girls and mothers to read together.

Mothering Ourselves: Help and Healing for Adult Daughters by Evelyn Bassoff (Dutton Plume, 1992). A guide to understanding how we were mothered and, as a result, how to better parent our own daughters.

Mothers and Daughters: Loving and Letting Go by Evelyn Bassoff (Dutton Plume, 1989). A loving and frank discussion of mothering girls—its conflicts, costs, and rewards—with special chapters on stepmothers and adoptive moms.

Our Daughters' Health: Practical and Invaluable Advice for Raising Confident Girls Ages 6-16 by Sharon L. Roan (Hyperion, 2001). Up-to-date information on the most common threats to a girl's well-being and what parents can do to protect her.

Our Last Best Shot: Guiding Our Children Through Early Adolescence by Laura Sessions Stepp (Putnam Publishing Group, 2000). Through the stories of 12 boys and girls across the United States, the author instructs parents on helping their children through the critical adolescent years.

Raising Their Voices: The Politics of Girls' Anger by Lyn Mikel Brown (Harvard University Press, 1999). A report on anger in girls' lives and the ways girls resist gender stereotypes.

Reviving Ophelia: Saving the Selves of Adolescent Girls by Mary Pipher (Ballantine Publishing Group, 1999). The landmark book that began the girls' movement. A powerful look at how our culture can destroy a girl's sense of self. Includes strategies that families can use to make her whole again.

The Romance of Risk: Why Teenagers Do the Things They Do by Lynn Ponton (Basic Books, 1998). Looks at how risk taking can be a tool that adolescents

use to define themselves and how parents can guide teens toward healthy risks.

See Jane Win: The Rimm Report on How 1,000 Girls Became Successful Women by Sylvia Rimm (Crown Publishing Group, 2000). Advice on raising girls for success, based on research into the childhood environments of women with careers in science, medicine, technology, law, the arts, education, and other fields.

The Sex Lives of Teenagers: Revealing the Secret World of Adolescent Boys and Girls by Lynn Ponton (Dutton Plume, 2000). Forthright anecdotes from the author's experience counseling young people about sexual feelings, experiences, and misconceptions. Includes discussions of sexual orientation and sexual violence.

SmartGirl.com. This Web site contains bulletin boards, surveys, and reviews, all written by girls ages 12 to 20. Discussion groups are reviewed regularly to keep them as free as possible of inappropriate content. Parents should note that SmartGirl sells research to clients, but girls' names or addresses are not included when aggregate information is distributed.

Stick Up for Yourself! Every Kid's Guide to Personal Power and Positive Self-Esteem by *Venus*

Gershen Kaufman, Lev Raphael, and Pamela Espeland (Free Spirit Publishing, 1999). Practical ways to help a girl use her voice.

Venus in Blue Jeans: Why Mothers and Daughters Need to Talk About Sex by Nathalie Bartle with Susan Lieberman (Houghton Mifflin Company, 1999). Helpful research about how much girls really know about sex (less than you think) and what parents need to tell them.

When Girls Feel Fat: Helping Girls Through Adolescence by Sandra Susan Friedman (HarperCollins Publishers, 2000). A thoughtful discussion of the feelings behind girls' weight issues. Suggests words you can use when talking with your daughter.

Will You Still Love Me If I Don't Win? A Guide for Parents of Young Athletes by Christopher Andersonn with Barbara Andersonn (Taylor Publishing Company, 2000). A thoughtful exploration of the emotional component of sports, including how we can help athletic children maintain balanced lives.

Associations

Eating Disorders
American Anorexia/Bulimia Association, Inc.
Offers information about eating disorders, counseling,
and support groups.
165 West 46th St., Suite 1108
New York, NY 10036
(212) 575-6200
www.aabainc.org

Eating Disorders Awareness and Prevention
Free information on eating disorders and referrals for treatment.
603 Stewart St., Suite 803
Seattle, WA 98101
(800) 931-2237

National Association of Anorexia Nervosa and Associated Disorders
A free resource offering a hotline, inpatient and outpatient referrals, and support groups in all 50 states and 14 countries.
P.O. Box 7
Highland Park, IL 60035
(847) 831-3438
www.anad.org

Physical and Mental Health
American Academy of Child and Adolescent Psychiatry
3615 Wisconsin Ave., N.W.
Washington, DC 20016-3007
(800) 333-7636
www.aacap.org

American Academy of Pediatrics
141 Northwest Point Blvd.
Elk Grove Village, IL 60007-1098
(847) 434-4000
www.aap.org

American Foundation for Suicide Prevention
Provides referrals and information

about depression and suicide, plus
support programs for survivors.
120 Wall St., 22nd Floor
New York, NY 10005
(212) 363-3500
www.afsp.org

School and Sports

Center for Adolescent Studies
Focuses on advancing the understanding of the psychological,
biological, and social features
of adolescence. Has links to
resources for parents.
School of Education
Indiana University
Bloomington, IN 47405-1006
(812) 856-8113
www.education.indiana.edu/cas/

*National Attention Deficit
Disorder Association*
Articles on treatment and coaching, research, support groups,
and legal news. Includes special
pages for kids with ADD.
1788 Second St., Suite 200
Highland Park, IL 60035
(847) 432-2332
www.add.org

Women's Sports Foundation
Eisenhower Park
East Meadow, NY 22554
(800) 227-3988
www.womenssportsfoundation.org

Substance Use and Abuse

Al-Anon/Alateen
Alateen offers resources for
teenagers whose lives have
been affected by someone else's
drinking.

Al-Anon Family Group
Headquarters
1600 Corporate Landing Pkwy.
Virginia Beach, VA 23454
(888) 4AL-ANON
www.al-anon-alateen.org

*American Council for Drug
Education*
Offers information on drug use
and pregnancy, the warning signs
of drug use, and tips for talking
with kids about drugs.
(800) 488-3784
www.acde.org

DrugHelp
A private, nonprofit information
and referral network providing
information on specific drugs,
treatment options, and family support groups. Offers a free, 24-
hour, confidential helpline.
(800) 662-HELP
www.drughelp.org

*National Center for Tobacco-
Free Kids*
1400 Eye Street, Suite 1200
Washington, DC 20005
(202) 296-5469
www.tobaccofreekids.org

*National Clearinghouse for
Alcohol and Drug Information*
Provides prevention and intervention information, research,
and a variety of publications. Part
of the U.S. Department of Health
and Human Services.
P.O. Box 2345
Rockville, MD 20847-2345
(800) 729-6686
www.health.org

Index

Help your daughter help herself with advice books from
American Girl Library®, written specifically for girls ages 8 to 12.

A Smart Girl's Guide to Boys: Surviving Crushes, Staying True to Yourself, and Other Love Stuff.

Caring advice on how to feel good and be yourself around boys. Letters, tips, and quizzes cover how to talk to a boy, what to do if he likes you, what to do if your friends like boys and you don't, and dealing with rejection. 112 pages. $9.95

Help! A Girl's Guide to Divorce and Stepfamilies.

When her parents break up, a girl's world can turn upside down. In this third title in the Help! series, American Girl answers letters on every aspect of divorce, from the initial split to a parent's remarriage. The book includes tips, quizzes, and advice from girls who've been there. Parents Choice award and National Parenting Publications award winner. 128 pages. $8.95

The Care and Keeping of Friends.

Heartfelt advice on how to make a friend, keep a friend, and be a friend. Conversation starters for when she's feeling shy, plus tips on staying close when a friend moves, fighting fair, and what to do when a friendship fades. 96 pages. $7.95

The Care and Keeping of You: The Body Book for Girls.

This "head-to-toe" guide answers all your daughter's questions, from hair care to healthy eating, bad breath to bras, periods to pimples. A national bestseller. 104 pages. $9.95

Good Sports: Winning. Losing. And Everything in Between.

A spirited playbook with advice on how to be a strong athlete both mentally and physically. Offers tips on improving skills, playing against friends and boys, dealing with coaches and parents—plus losing with grace and winning with pride. Parents Choice award winner. 96 pages. $8.95

Oh, Brother . . . Oh, Sister! A Sister's Guide to Getting Along.

Having a brother or sister (or several!) can be both a joy and a pain. Here's practical advice on issues brothers and sisters face, including fighting, sharing, jealousy, and respect. Tips, quizzes, and special extras help make family life easier. 64 pages. $7.95

For more information, visit the bookstore at www.americangirl.com.